# Historical Records of Maritime Tragedies

Shah Rukh

Published by Shah Rukh, 2024.

While every precaution has been taken in the preparation of this book, the publisher assumes no responsibility for errors or omissions, or for damages resulting from the use of the information contained herein.

HISTORICAL RECORDS OF MARITIME TRAGEDIES

**First edition. June 16, 2024.**

Copyright © 2024 Shah Rukh.

Written by Shah Rukh.

# Table of Contents

# Prologue

The ocean, vast and enigmatic, has long been a source of fascination, inspiration, and fear. It covers over seventy percent of our planet, a realm of untamed beauty and unpredictable peril. For centuries, humanity has ventured into its depths, driven by curiosity, trade, exploration, and conquest. Yet, the sea remains a formidable adversary, indifferent to human ambition and endeavor. It has witnessed countless tales of bravery, tragedy, and mystery, many of which have been etched into the annals of maritime history.

This book, "Historical Records of Maritime Tragedies," delves into fifty of the most compelling and harrowing incidents ever recorded. Each chapter reveals a story of ships lost to the depths, crews vanished without a trace, and vessels destroyed by the elements or human error. These accounts span the globe and the centuries, from the earliest days of seafaring to modern times, highlighting the enduring dangers of the maritime world.

As you turn these pages, you will journey back to the frigid waters of the North Atlantic, where the "unsinkable" Titanic met its tragic end. You will stand on the decks of the HMS Hood as it faces its fateful encounter with the Bismarck. You will ponder the eerie abandonment of the Mary Celeste and the mysterious disappearance of the USS Cyclops in the Bermuda Triangle. Each story is a testament to the ocean's power to humble even the most advanced ships and the most experienced sailors.

These tales are not just chronicles of loss; they are also stories of survival, heroism, and the relentless human spirit. They remind us of the bravery of those who face the sea's perils and the enduring hope that drives search and rescue missions long after hope seems lost. They also serve as a sobering reminder of the ocean's might, urging us to respect and understand its vast, unpredictable nature.

"Historical Records of Maritime Tragedies" is a tribute to those who have sailed the seas and to the many who have met their fate beneath the waves. It is an exploration of the ocean's darker side, a side filled with unanswered questions and tragic tales. As we embark on this journey through maritime history, we pay homage to the sailors, passengers, and ships that have been claimed by the sea, and we reflect on the lessons they leave behind.

Welcome aboard, and may these stories stir your imagination, evoke your compassion, and deepen your respect for the mighty oceans that both give life and take it away.

# Chapter 1: Titanic

The sinking of the RMS Titanic in 1912 stands as one of the most infamous maritime disasters in history, embodying a tragic confluence of human ambition, technological hubris, and natural forces. The Titanic was the pride of the White Star Line, a British shipping company eager to dominate the transatlantic passenger trade. Launched from the Harland and Wolff shipyard in Belfast, Northern Ireland, Titanic was heralded as the largest and most luxurious ocean liner ever built, designed with state-of-the-art safety features and deemed "practically unsinkable."

On April 10, 1912, the Titanic set sail on her maiden voyage from Southampton, England, to New York City. The ship's passenger list included a cross-section of society, from wealthy industrialists and socialites to immigrants seeking a new life in America. Prominent passengers included John Jacob Astor IV, one of the wealthiest men in America; Isidor Straus, co-owner of Macy's department store; and Margaret "Molly" Brown, later celebrated for her acts of heroism during the disaster.

Titanic's design was a marvel of early 20th-century engineering. The ship was 882 feet long, had a gross tonnage of 46,328, and boasted a range of luxurious accommodations. First-class passengers enjoyed opulent staterooms, a grand staircase, a swimming pool, and gourmet dining. Second-class accommodations, though less extravagant, were still comfortable, while third-class passengers, many of whom were emigrants, traveled in more modest but nonetheless adequate quarters. The ship's advanced safety features included a double-bottomed hull and watertight compartments intended to prevent the vessel from sinking even if several compartments were breached.

Despite its impressive construction, the Titanic was fatally flawed. One critical oversight was the number of lifeboats. Regulations at the time did not require a sufficient number for all passengers and crew, and Titanic carried only 20 lifeboats, enough for about half of those on board. This decision was influenced by aesthetic concerns and the mistaken belief in the ship's unsinkability. Additionally, the ship's watertight compartments were not capped at the top, allowing water to spill from one to the next in a cascading effect.

On the night of April 14, 1912, the Titanic was steaming through the North Atlantic at near full speed despite several ice warnings from other ships in the area. The night was clear but moonless, making it difficult to spot icebergs. At 11:40 p.m., lookouts Frederick Fleet and Reginald Lee sighted an iceberg directly ahead. First Officer William Murdoch ordered the ship to turn hard to port and reverse the engines, but the iceberg was too close. The Titanic scraped along the side of the iceberg, creating a series of punctures below the waterline.

The iceberg caused the hull plates to buckle and allowed water to flood five of the ship's forward compartments. Captain Edward Smith, after assessing the damage with shipbuilder Thomas Andrews, realized that the Titanic was doomed. The flooding of so many compartments meant the bow would sink lower, causing water to spill over into each subsequent compartment. The ship was estimated to stay afloat for no more than a couple of hours.

A distress call was sent out, and the nearby ship Carpathia, about 58 miles away, raced to the scene. However, Carpathia would not arrive in time to prevent a catastrophe. The evacuation process was chaotic and insufficiently organized. Lifeboats were launched half-full due to a lack of clear instructions and the disbelief that the ship was sinking. Women and children were given priority for the lifeboats, but many seats went empty as the crew struggled with the deployment.

As the Titanic's bow sank deeper, passengers experienced a surreal and horrifying scene. The ship's orchestra, led by Wallace Hartley, famously played on the deck to calm the panicked crowd. Survivors later recounted hearing the strains of "Nearer, My God, to Thee" as the ship met its fate. The stern of the Titanic lifted high into the air before breaking apart, and at 2:20 a.m. on April 15, the ship disappeared beneath the icy waters of the Atlantic.

Of the 2,224 people on board, more than 1,500 perished in the disaster. Many succumbed to hypothermia in the freezing water, while others were trapped inside the sinking ship. The survivors, numbering about 710, were eventually rescued by the Carpathia. The loss of life was catastrophic and led to an international outcry and a subsequent overhaul of maritime safety regulations. The disaster prompted the establishment of the International Ice Patrol to monitor iceberg activity and the requirement for sufficient lifeboats on all ships, among other safety measures.

The sinking of the Titanic has since captured the imagination of the public and has been the subject of numerous books, films, and documentaries. The wreck was discovered in 1985 by a team led by oceanographer Robert Ballard, lying over 12,000 feet below the surface of the Atlantic. The discovery sparked new interest in the tragedy, providing valuable insights into the ship's final moments and reigniting debates over the ethical considerations of salvaging artifacts from the site.

The Titanic disaster is often seen as a poignant symbol of human arrogance and the limitations of technology. It underscores the fragility of human endeavor in the face of nature's vast and uncontrollable forces. The tragedy has left an indelible mark on popular culture and collective memory, serving as a sobering reminder of the perils of overconfidence and the importance of vigilance and preparedness in maritime travel.

# Chapter 2: HMS Hood

The HMS Hood, a British battlecruiser of the Royal Navy, was one of the most iconic warships of the 20th century and its dramatic sinking in 1941 during World War II stands as a poignant chapter in maritime history. Named after the 18th-century admiral Samuel Hood, HMS Hood was commissioned in 1920 and represented the zenith of British naval power between the World Wars. It was the last of the Admiral-class battlecruisers, designed as a formidable symbol of the Royal Navy's might and a response to the rise of other naval powers.

HMS Hood was conceived during World War I but was completed in the post-war period. At the time of its launch, it was the largest warship in the world, measuring 860 feet in length with a displacement of over 42,000 tons. Its speed, armament, and size earned it the nickname "The Mighty Hood." The ship's design reflected the transitional nature of naval architecture in the early 20th century, blending elements of both battleships and battlecruisers. It was equipped with eight 15-inch guns in four twin turrets, making it a powerful adversary against other capital ships. The secondary armament included twelve 5.5-inch guns and eight 4-inch anti-aircraft guns, complemented by torpedo tubes.

Despite its impressive size and firepower, the HMS Hood had notable vulnerabilities. Its armor protection, particularly on the deck, was insufficient against plunging fire from enemy battleships and modern naval guns. The ship's initial design flaws were partly due to the hasty decisions made during its construction, as it was intended to counter the threat of the German High Seas Fleet. Efforts to modernize the Hood and enhance its protection were repeatedly delayed due to budget constraints and the advent of newer ships, resulting in the battlecruiser retaining many of its original weaknesses throughout its service.

Throughout the interwar period, HMS Hood served as the flagship of the Royal Navy's battlecruiser squadron and embarked on numerous deployments, including goodwill tours to show British naval power globally. The ship's majestic silhouette became a symbol of British maritime dominance, and it played a vital role in the projection of power across the British Empire. The Hood was also involved in various international events, including the Spithead Review in 1935, which celebrated King George V's Silver Jubilee and showcased the Royal Navy's strength.

With the outbreak of World War II in 1939, HMS Hood's role became even more crucial. The ship participated in operations to intercept German raiders and protect Allied shipping in the North Atlantic. Its formidable reputation, however, faced a significant test in May 1941, when it was assigned to intercept the German battleship Bismarck and the heavy cruiser Prinz Eugen, which had set sail from Norway on a mission to disrupt Allied supply lines. The ensuing naval engagement, known as the Battle of the Denmark Strait, would lead to one of the most dramatic and tragic moments in naval history.

On May 24, 1941, HMS Hood, alongside the battleship HMS Prince of Wales, encountered Bismarck and Prinz Eugen in the Denmark Strait, between Greenland and Iceland. The British forces, commanded by Vice-Admiral Lancelot Holland, aimed to stop the German ships before they could break out into the North Atlantic. The battle commenced early in the morning under challenging conditions, with poor visibility and rough seas complicating the engagement. The Hood, leading the British formation, opened fire on the German ships, initially targeting Prinz Eugen by mistake due to the confusing weather conditions.

As the battle progressed, the British ships adjusted their fire to engage Bismarck. Despite the disparity in armor protection, the Hood's initial volleys failed to significantly damage the German battleship. The Bismarck, under the command of Admiral Günther

Lütjens and Captain Ernst Lindemann, returned fire with devastating accuracy. Within minutes, a critical hit from Bismarck's 15-inch shells struck the Hood, penetrating its relatively thin deck armor and reaching the aft magazine. The resulting explosion was catastrophic, causing the ship to break in two and sink within minutes. The violent destruction of HMS Hood led to the loss of 1,415 of its 1,418 crew members, including Vice-Admiral Holland. Only three men survived the sinking, clinging to debris until they were rescued by the destroyer HMS Electra.

The loss of HMS Hood sent shockwaves throughout Britain and the Allied nations. The ship had been a symbol of British naval supremacy, and its destruction by the Bismarck, a relatively new and powerful German battleship, represented a significant blow to British morale. The tragedy galvanized the Royal Navy to launch an intensive pursuit of the Bismarck, culminating in the German battleship's own destruction on May 27, 1941, after being relentlessly hunted and engaged by British forces. This episode, known as the "Hunt for the Bismarck," underscored the Royal Navy's determination to avenge the loss of the Hood and eliminate a significant threat to Allied naval operations.

In the aftermath of the sinking, there were numerous inquiries and debates regarding the reasons behind the Hood's rapid demise. Investigations highlighted the inadequacies in the ship's design, particularly its armor protection and vulnerability to plunging fire. The battle also underscored the evolving nature of naval warfare, where airpower and more heavily armored ships began to dominate the strategic landscape. The lessons learned from the Hood's destruction influenced future naval design and tactics, emphasizing the need for better protection and adaptability to modern threats.

The wreck of HMS Hood was discovered in 2001 by an expedition led by David Mearns, an underwater explorer and maritime historian. The wreckage lies at a depth of approximately 2,800 meters in the

Denmark Strait, scattered across the ocean floor in pieces due to the force of the explosion and the impact with the seabed. The discovery provided valuable insights into the ship's final moments and has served as a poignant reminder of the sacrifices made by those who served aboard the Hood.

HMS Hood's legacy continues to resonate in naval history and popular culture. The ship's story has been the subject of numerous books, documentaries, and memorials. It stands as a symbol of both the power and the vulnerability of naval warfare, reflecting the complex interplay of technology, strategy, and human endeavor. The tragic fate of HMS Hood serves as a somber reminder of the perils faced by those who go to sea in defense of their nations and the enduring impact of maritime conflict on history.

# Chapter 3: Mary Celeste

The mystery of the Mary Celeste remains one of the most enduring and intriguing maritime enigmas of the 19th century. The ship, an American merchant brigantine, was discovered adrift and deserted in the Atlantic Ocean on December 5, 1872. Its crew had vanished without a trace, leaving behind a vessel in seemingly seaworthy condition with a cargo intact. Over the years, numerous theories and speculations have emerged to explain the circumstances surrounding the disappearance, but the fate of the Mary Celeste's crew remains an unresolved mystery.

The Mary Celeste was built in Spencer's Island, Nova Scotia, and was originally christened the Amazon in 1861. The ship was a two-masted brigantine measuring 103 feet in length with a tonnage of 282 tons. Over the course of its early career, the vessel faced several incidents, including a collision and a change in ownership. In 1869, the ship was acquired by a group of American investors, underwent significant repairs and refitting, and was renamed the Mary Celeste. By the time of its fateful voyage in 1872, the vessel was under the command of Captain Benjamin Briggs, an experienced and respected seaman.

Captain Briggs was accompanied by his wife, Sarah, their two-year-old daughter, Sophia, and a crew of seven experienced sailors. The Mary Celeste set sail from New York City on November 7, 1872, bound for Genoa, Italy, carrying a cargo of 1,701 barrels of denatured alcohol. The journey began uneventfully, with Captain Briggs maintaining a logbook that recorded daily events and the ship's position.

On December 5, 1872, the British brigantine Dei Gratia, under the command of Captain David Morehouse, sighted the Mary Celeste adrift and seemingly abandoned about 400 miles east of the Azores. The Dei Gratia's crew boarded the vessel and found it deserted, with no sign of Captain Briggs, his family, or the crew. The ship's last log entry was dated November 25, 1872, placing the Mary Celeste near Santa Maria Island in the Azores, indicating that the ship had been drifting for approximately ten days.

The condition of the Mary Celeste when it was discovered has fueled endless speculation and theories. The ship was found in a relatively seaworthy state, with the sails partially set and some of them damaged. The lifeboat was missing, suggesting that it had been launched, but there was no clear reason why the crew would have abandoned the ship in such a hurry. Personal belongings, including valuable items, were left behind, indicating that whatever prompted the abandonment was sudden and unexpected.

The cargo of denatured alcohol was largely intact, with only nine barrels found empty. The ship's hold was flooded with about three and a half feet of water, but this was not enough to endanger the vessel. The ship's compasses were found to be damaged, and the navigational instruments and ship's papers, except for the logbook, were missing. The food supply was sufficient for six months, and the ship's provisions were untouched, further deepening the mystery.

Theories to explain the disappearance of the Mary Celeste's crew range from plausible to outlandish. One of the more credible theories suggests that the crew may have abandoned ship due to fears of an explosion. The cargo of denatured alcohol, which is highly volatile, could have leaked and created dangerous fumes. If the crew suspected an imminent explosion, they might have hastily abandoned the ship, possibly planning to return once the danger had passed. However, the lifeboat was never found, and there were no signs of an explosion or fire on the ship.

Another theory posits that the crew encountered a severe weather event, such as a waterspout or a sudden seaquake, which may have caused a temporary panic. The ship's waterlogged condition and damaged rigging suggest that it may have faced rough weather. If the crew believed the ship was in immediate danger, they might have evacuated in the lifeboat, intending to return once the storm passed. This theory, however, does not account for why they would not have taken essential navigation equipment and personal belongings.

Piracy has also been considered as a potential explanation, though this theory is less supported by evidence. The intact state of the cargo and the absence of any signs of struggle or violence make it unlikely that pirates were responsible. Moreover, pirates typically sought valuable goods, and there was no evidence of theft or looting.

Mutiny and foul play among the crew have also been suggested, though there is no concrete evidence to support these claims. The crew members were experienced sailors, and there was no indication of discord or conflict prior to their disappearance. Captain Briggs was known to be a capable and well-respected commander, making mutiny an unlikely scenario.

More exotic and speculative theories include the possibility of paranormal events or supernatural phenomena, such as the intervention of a sea monster or alien abduction. These ideas, while captivating to the imagination, lack any scientific or factual basis and are generally considered the realm of fiction rather than serious inquiry.

The discovery of the Mary Celeste created a sensation in both maritime and popular circles, leading to numerous investigations and court proceedings. The ship was brought to Gibraltar, where an inquiry was conducted to determine the circumstances of the abandonment. The inquiry, led by Frederick Solly-Flood, the Attorney General of Gibraltar, initially suspected foul play but eventually concluded that the evidence was inconclusive, and the fate of the crew remained a mystery.

The Mary Celeste continued to sail under different owners and names until its final demise in 1885. The ship was deliberately wrecked off the coast of Haiti in an attempt to commit insurance fraud, but the scheme was discovered, and the vessel was abandoned to the elements.

The wreck of the Mary Celeste was rediscovered in 2001 by marine archaeologist Clive Cussler, adding a final chapter to its storied and enigmatic history.

The tale of the Mary Celeste has been immortalized in literature, film, and popular culture, captivating the imagination of generations. The ship's mysterious abandonment remains one of the most compelling maritime puzzles, evoking a sense of intrigue and wonder that continues to inspire speculation and debate. The unanswered questions surrounding the Mary Celeste's fate serve as a reminder of the enduring mysteries of the sea and the limits of human understanding in the face of the vast and unpredictable forces of nature.

# Chapter 4: USS Indianapolis

The story of the USS Indianapolis, a Portland-class heavy cruiser of the United States Navy, is one of the most tragic and dramatic episodes in naval history, particularly during World War II. The ship's final mission in 1945 and its subsequent sinking resulted in one of the worst maritime disasters in U.S. naval history. This event is notable not only for the significant loss of life but also for the critical nature of its final mission and the harrowing experiences of its survivors. The saga of the USS Indianapolis encompasses themes of bravery, survival, and the stark realities of war, leaving an indelible mark on naval history and collective memory.

Commissioned in 1932, the USS Indianapolis was one of two Portland-class cruisers, characterized by its 610-foot length, a displacement of over 9,800 tons, and a top speed of 32 knots. Armed with nine 8-inch guns, eight 5-inch anti-aircraft guns, and several anti-aircraft machine guns, the Indianapolis was a formidable vessel designed for both offensive and defensive operations. Throughout its service, the ship played significant roles in various naval engagements and missions during World War II, including operations in the Pacific Theater.

One of the USS Indianapolis' most notable roles occurred in the closing days of World War II. In July 1945, the ship was tasked with a highly secretive and critical mission: to deliver components of the atomic bomb, "Little Boy," to the island of Tinian in the Pacific. This bomb would later be dropped on Hiroshima, contributing to the end of the war. The successful delivery of these components marked the culmination of the Manhattan Project's efforts to develop an atomic weapon and underscored the Indianapolis' significant contribution to the war effort.

After completing its mission at Tinian, the Indianapolis was ordered to proceed to Leyte in the Philippines to prepare for further operations. However, on the night of July 30, 1945, while en route to Leyte, the ship was torpedoed by the Japanese submarine I-58 under the command of Lieutenant Commander Mochitsura Hashimoto. The attack occurred shortly after midnight, when the Indianapolis was approximately halfway between Guam and Leyte, in an area known as the Philippine Sea. The submarine launched a spread of six torpedoes, two of which struck the Indianapolis with devastating effect.

The first torpedo hit the forward part of the ship, causing a massive explosion that severed the bow and ignited a fire. The second torpedo struck near the middle of the ship, causing catastrophic damage to the fuel tanks and boiler rooms. The explosions created an inferno, and the ship began to list rapidly to starboard. The damage was so severe and sudden that the ship sank within 12 minutes of the attack. Out of a crew of 1,195, approximately 300 sailors went down with the ship. The remaining 900 men were cast into the open sea, many with only life jackets or makeshift flotation devices.

The ordeal of the survivors in the water is a harrowing tale of endurance and suffering. They were left adrift in shark-infested waters for four days, battling exposure, dehydration, and the constant threat of shark attacks. The initial hope of a quick rescue faded as time went on and no help arrived. The lack of an SOS signal and the secrecy surrounding the ship's mission contributed to the delay in rescue operations, as the ship's disappearance went unnoticed for several days. Compounding this, a series of communication errors and misunderstandings led to the failure to launch a timely search and rescue mission.

The men faced brutal conditions in the water. Many suffered from severe burns, injuries, and saltwater ingestion, leading to hallucinations and insanity. Sharks, drawn by the noise and commotion, attacked the defenseless men, causing additional casualties. The survivors clung to debris and each other, forming small groups to increase their chances of survival. They faced extreme dehydration, resorting to drinking seawater out of desperation, which led to further suffering and, in some cases, death.

It wasn't until August 2, 1945, that the survivors were accidentally spotted by a PV-1 Ventura aircraft piloted by Lieutenant Wilbur Gwinn. Gwinn, who was on a routine patrol, noticed an oil slick and later saw the men in the water. He immediately radioed for assistance, initiating a rescue operation. A PBY Catalina seaplane, piloted by Lieutenant Commander Robert Adrian Marks, was dispatched to the area. Upon arrival, Marks disobeyed orders by landing in the open ocean to save as many men as possible, despite the risk of damaging his plane. He managed to rescue 56 men directly from the water.

The rescue continued with the arrival of the USS Cecil J. Doyle, which responded to the distress call and began picking up survivors. Over the next few days, additional ships joined the rescue efforts, eventually saving a total of 316 men. The survivors were taken to Guam and then to hospitals for treatment, where they received medical care for their injuries and trauma. The ordeal left an indelible mark on the survivors, many of whom suffered from long-term physical and psychological effects.

The aftermath of the USS Indianapolis tragedy sparked significant controversy and led to an inquiry into the circumstances surrounding the ship's loss. Captain Charles B. McVay III, the commanding officer of the Indianapolis, was court-martialed and convicted of failing to order the crew to abandon ship in a timely manner and for failing to zigzag, a maneuver intended to evade submarine attacks. The court-martial was highly controversial, with many believing that McVay was unfairly scapegoated for the disaster. In 2000, after years of advocacy by survivors and their families, Captain McVay was posthumously exonerated by an act of Congress, acknowledging that he had been wrongly blamed for the ship's sinking.

The sinking of the USS Indianapolis remains a profound lesson in the dangers of war and the complexities of naval operations. The event highlighted issues such as the need for better communication and coordination in rescue operations, the importance of adequate lifeboats and survival equipment, and the psychological toll of extended survival in extreme conditions. The bravery and resilience of the Indianapolis' crew, both during the attack and in the days that followed, stand as a testament to the human spirit in the face of unimaginable adversity.

The story of the USS Indianapolis has been commemorated in various forms of media, including books, documentaries, and films, which have helped to keep the memory of the tragedy alive. The ship's fate and the suffering of its crew continue to resonate as a poignant reminder of the sacrifices made during wartime and the enduring impact of such events on those who serve and their families. The legacy of the USS Indianapolis endures as a symbol of both the heroism and the horror that characterize the human experience in times of conflict.

# Chapter 5: Andrea Doria

The Andrea Doria, an Italian ocean liner, is one of the most famous and tragic maritime disasters of the 20th century. Launched in 1951 and named after the 16th-century Genoese admiral Andrea Doria, the ship was a symbol of post-war Italian pride and technological achievement. It was celebrated for its luxurious accommodations, state-of-the-art safety features, and artistic elegance, often described as a floating palace. Despite its modern design and amenities, the Andrea Doria met a tragic end in 1956 when it collided with the Swedish passenger liner MS Stockholm. This collision resulted in the Andrea Doria's sinking and marked one of the worst peacetime maritime disasters.

The Andrea Doria was built by the Italian Line (Italia Società per Azioni di Navigazione) at the Ansaldo shipyard in Genoa. The ship was intended to compete with other prestigious transatlantic liners and to restore Italy's presence in the post-war ocean liner market. It measured 697 feet in length, had a beam of 90 feet, and a gross tonnage of 29,083 tons. The ship could accommodate around 1,200 passengers and a crew of 500, divided into three classes: first, cabin, and tourist.

The Andrea Doria's interior was a testament to Italian craftsmanship and design. The ship featured luxurious public spaces adorned with murals, sculptures, and art pieces by renowned Italian artists such as Salvatore Fiume and Giulio Rosso. The first-class section included a swimming pool, ballroom, and numerous dining areas, all designed to provide passengers with a comfortable and opulent journey across the Atlantic. The ship was also equipped with advanced safety features for its time, including a double hull, multiple watertight compartments, and the latest radar technology.

On July 25, 1956, the Andrea Doria was on the final leg of a voyage from Genoa to New York City, carrying 1,134 passengers and 572 crew members. The ship was under the command of Captain Piero Calamai, an experienced seaman with a distinguished career. The voyage had been largely uneventful, and the ship was expected to arrive in New York the following morning. However, the weather had deteriorated as the ship approached the coast of the United States, with heavy fog reducing visibility.

Meanwhile, the MS Stockholm, a Swedish passenger liner operated by the Swedish American Line, was departing New York for its return voyage to Gothenburg, Sweden. The Stockholm was a smaller ship, measuring 525 feet in length with a gross tonnage of 12,165 tons, and capable of carrying around 600 passengers. It was under the command of Captain Gunnar Nordenson, who was not on the bridge at the time of the collision. The ship's third officer, Johan-Ernst Carstens-Johannsen, was in command and navigating through the dense fog, relying on radar to detect nearby ships.

At around 11:10 PM, approximately 45 miles south of Nantucket Island, Massachusetts, the Andrea Doria and the Stockholm were on a collision course. Both ships were aware of each other's presence through radar but misinterpreted each other's positions and movements. The Andrea Doria, traveling at 21.8 knots, was approaching from the west, while the Stockholm, moving at 18.5 knots, was heading east. The confusion was compounded by the fact that both ships were operating under the belief that the other would alter its course to avoid a collision, a standard maritime practice known as the "rules of the road."

Due to the heavy fog, visibility was extremely poor, and the radar readings were misinterpreted. The Andrea Doria was initially thought to be on a parallel course with the Stockholm, while the Stockholm's officers believed the Andrea Doria was further to the east. The Andrea Doria's crew decided to turn to port, intending to pass the Stockholm on the starboard side. However, the Stockholm's crew made a similar decision, also turning to port, leading to an imminent collision.

At 11:10 PM, the Stockholm's bow collided with the starboard side of the Andrea Doria. The impact created a massive gash in the Andrea Doria's hull, extending from below the waterline to the upper decks. The collision penetrated several watertight compartments, causing the ship to list heavily to starboard. The Stockholm's reinforced ice-breaking bow, designed to navigate through icy waters, acted like a giant knife, slicing through the Andrea Doria's side and causing catastrophic damage. The Stockholm, although damaged, remained afloat and was able to assist in the rescue efforts.

The Andrea Doria began to list at an alarming rate, making it difficult to launch lifeboats on the port side. The ship's crew and passengers were thrown into chaos, with many trapped in their cabins or struggling to make their way to the lifeboats. Despite the severe damage and the rapidly worsening situation, the Andrea Doria's crew, led by Captain Calamai, attempted to maintain order and organize an evacuation.

The distress signal sent out by the Andrea Doria was picked up by numerous nearby ships, including the French liner Île de France, which played a crucial role in the rescue operation. The Île de France, under the command of Captain Raoul de Beaudéan, was one of the first ships to arrive at the scene, and its crew worked tirelessly to rescue survivors. Other vessels, such as the Cape Ann, the Robert E. Hopkins, and the USNS Private William H. Thomas, also responded to the distress call and participated in the rescue efforts.

The evacuation was hampered by the Andrea Doria's severe list, which made it difficult to launch lifeboats on the starboard side. Nonetheless, the crew and rescuers managed to launch enough lifeboats to save most of the passengers. The Stockholm also assisted in the rescue; despite the damage it sustained in the collision. Many of the Andrea Doria's passengers were taken aboard the Île de France, which provided medical assistance and comfort to the survivors.

The rescue operation continued throughout the night and into the early hours of July 26. By dawn, nearly all of the Andrea Doria's passengers and crew had been rescued. Tragically, 46 people aboard the Andrea Doria lost their lives, either in the initial collision or in the aftermath. The ship continued to list and eventually capsized and sank at 10:09 AM on July 26, 1956, disappearing beneath the waves and coming to rest on the seabed at a depth of approximately 240 feet.

The collision between the Andrea Doria and the Stockholm prompted a thorough investigation into the causes of the disaster. The inquiry revealed several contributing factors, including navigational errors, poor visibility, and misinterpretation of radar readings. Both ships were found to have made critical mistakes in their navigation and communication, leading to the tragic collision. The investigation also highlighted the need for improvements in maritime safety regulations, particularly regarding radar operation and the rules for navigating in poor visibility.

The sinking of the Andrea Doria had a significant impact on the maritime industry and public perception of ocean liner travel. The disaster led to changes in safety protocols, including improved radar training for ship officers and stricter regulations for navigating in foggy conditions. The incident also marked a turning point in the decline of ocean liner travel, as air travel became increasingly popular and more accessible.

The wreck of the Andrea Doria has since become a popular site for scuba divers, often referred to as the "Mount Everest of diving" due to the challenging conditions and the historical significance of the wreck. Over the years, numerous expeditions have explored the wreck, recovering artifacts and documenting the ship's condition. The wreck lies on its starboard side at a depth of around 240 feet, with much of the ship's structure still intact. The site remains a testament to the tragedy and serves as a reminder of the importance of maritime safety and the ever-present dangers of sea travel.

The story of the Andrea Doria has been immortalized in books, documentaries, and films, capturing the dramatic events of that fateful night and the heroic efforts of those involved in the rescue. The disaster continues to captivate the imagination and stands as a poignant chapter in maritime history, reflecting both the achievements and the vulnerabilities of human endeavor in the face of the unpredictable forces of nature. The legacy of the Andrea Doria endures as a symbol of the fragility of life at sea and the enduring impact of maritime tragedies on our collective consciousness.

# Chapter 6: MV Wilhelm Gustloff

The MV Wilhelm Gustloff is a name that echoes through the annals of maritime history as the site of one of the deadliest maritime disasters in human history. Launched in 1937, the ship was originally built as a cruise ship for the Nazi German organization Kraft durch Freude (Strength Through Joy), designed to promote leisure activities for the German working class. However, the ship's most infamous chapter unfolded during the final months of World War II, when it was repurposed for a desperate evacuation mission. The sinking of the Wilhelm Gustloff on January 30, 1945, resulted in the loss of over 9,000 lives, making it the largest loss of life in a single shipwreck, surpassing even the tragic fate of the RMS Titanic.

The Wilhelm Gustloff was named after Wilhelm Gustloff, the assassinated leader of the Nazi Party's Swiss branch. The ship, measuring 684 feet in length and with a gross tonnage of 25,484 tons, was a symbol of Nazi Germany's prowess and a tool for propaganda. Designed to provide affordable vacations to German workers, the ship boasted amenities such as a swimming pool, theaters, and dining halls, offering an experience that many of its passengers had never before enjoyed. Its pre-war voyages took Germans to various Mediterranean and North Sea destinations, promoting the image of a rejuvenated and prosperous Germany under Nazi rule.

With the onset of World War II, the Wilhelm Gustloff's role changed dramatically. In September 1939, the ship was requisitioned by the Kriegsmarine (German Navy) and converted into a hospital ship. It served in this capacity for the first few years of the war, treating wounded soldiers from various fronts. In 1940, as the nature of the war evolved and the need for hospital ships decreased, the Wilhelm Gustloff was again repurposed, this time as a floating barracks for the 2nd Submarine Training Division stationed in the Baltic Sea. The ship remained docked in the port city of Gotenhafen (now Gdynia, Poland) for much of the war, serving as stationary quarters for naval personnel.

By late 1944 and early 1945, the situation on the Eastern Front had deteriorated drastically for Nazi Germany. The Red Army was advancing westward, reclaiming territories occupied by the Germans and causing widespread panic among German civilians and military personnel alike. In East Prussia, Pomerania, and the Baltic States, hundreds of thousands of people were desperate to flee the approaching Soviet forces, who were infamous for their brutal reprisals against Germans as they advanced. Operation Hannibal was launched by the German Navy in January 1945, with the objective of evacuating German troops and civilians from these areas via the Baltic Sea.

The Wilhelm Gustloff, anchored in Gotenhafen, was one of the ships assigned to participate in this massive evacuation effort. The ship's intended capacity was for approximately 1,800 passengers, but on January 30, 1945, it was loaded far beyond its limits. Official records list the number of passengers as 6,050, including military personnel, wounded soldiers, members of the Women's Auxiliary Naval Service, and civilians, primarily women, children, and the elderly. However, subsequent estimates suggest that the actual number of people aboard was closer to 10,000, due to the sheer chaos and lack of accurate accounting during the boarding process.

As the Wilhelm Gustloff departed Gotenhafen, it faced treacherous winter conditions and the ever-present threat of enemy action. The ship was designed to be a leisure liner, not an icebreaker, and the Baltic Sea was filled with dangerous ice floes. Additionally, Soviet submarines were patrolling the area, hunting for German ships. The Wilhelm Gustloff was escorted by a few small vessels, but its sheer size and the crowded conditions made it a prominent and vulnerable target.

At around 8:00 PM on the night of January 30, 1945, the Wilhelm Gustloff was detected by the Soviet submarine S-13, commanded by

Captain Alexander Marinesko. Marinesko, known for his aggressive tactics and keen eye for targets, had been seeking an opportunity to make a significant impact against the German forces. The Wilhelm Gustloff, with its lights on and moving slowly through the ice-laden waters, presented itself as an ideal target.

At 9:16 PM, S-13 fired a spread of three torpedoes at the Wilhelm Gustloff from a range of approximately 3,000 yards. All three torpedoes hit their mark. The first torpedo struck the ship near the bow, causing a massive explosion that shattered the watertight compartments and sent water flooding into the lower decks. The second torpedo hit midship, causing further catastrophic damage and knocking out the ship's electrical systems. The third torpedo struck near the stern, destroying the ship's propulsion system and leaving it dead in the water.

The impact of the torpedoes caused immediate panic among the passengers and crew. The ship began to list rapidly, making it difficult for people to reach the lifeboats, many of which were frozen to their davits and could not be deployed. The freezing temperatures, estimated to be around -10°C (14°F), exacerbated the situation, with passengers struggling to survive in the icy water. Those who managed to escape the initial blast faced a grim fate, as hypothermia set in within minutes in the freezing Baltic Sea.

The chaos on board was unimaginable. Women and children were trampled in the rush to the lifeboats, and many were trapped below decks as the ship quickly filled with water. The few lifeboats that were successfully launched were overcrowded and barely able to stay afloat. The ship's list made it nearly impossible to launch lifeboats from the starboard side, and the port side was similarly compromised. Many passengers clung to debris or makeshift rafts, desperately trying to stay above water as the ship began to sink.

The Wilhelm Gustloff sank within 70 minutes of the torpedo strike, taking with it an estimated 9,400 people. The exact number of casualties remains uncertain due to the lack of accurate passenger records and the chaotic nature of the evacuation. The majority of the victims were civilians, including thousands of children who had been evacuated from the besieged eastern territories. The sinking of the Wilhelm Gustloff is often cited as the deadliest maritime disaster in history, with a death toll significantly higher than that of the Titanic or the Lusitania.

The aftermath of the disaster saw a limited number of survivors rescued by nearby vessels, including the German torpedo boat T-36 and the minesweeper M-387. These ships braved the treacherous conditions and the threat of further attacks to pull survivors from the frigid waters. The survivors were taken to ports in Germany and occupied Denmark, where they received medical treatment and care for their injuries and trauma. The sinking of the Wilhelm Gustloff left a profound impact on those who lived through the ordeal, with many survivors suffering from long-term physical and psychological effects.

The sinking of the Wilhelm Gustloff has been the subject of extensive historical analysis, debate, and reflection. It serves as a stark reminder of the horrors of war and the suffering endured by civilians caught in the crossfire. The disaster is often framed within the broader context of the brutal final months of World War II, highlighting the desperate measures taken by both Axis and Allied forces as the conflict drew to a close. The tragedy also underscores the complexities of historical memory, with the victims of the Wilhelm Gustloff representing a wide spectrum of experiences and identities, including civilians, military personnel, and refugees.

In the years following the war, the story of the Wilhelm Gustloff was often overshadowed by other wartime narratives, particularly those focusing on the atrocities committed by the Nazi regime. However, in recent decades, there has been a renewed interest in the disaster, with historians, writers, and filmmakers exploring the human dimensions of the tragedy and its place in the larger tapestry of World War II history.

The sinking of the Wilhelm Gustloff has been the subject of numerous books, documentaries, and academic studies, each contributing to a deeper understanding of the event and its lasting significance.

The wreck of the Wilhelm Gustloff lies at a depth of approximately 45 meters (150 feet) in the Baltic Sea, off the coast of Poland. The site is protected under Polish law as a war grave, recognizing the thousands of lives lost in the disaster. The wreck remains a somber reminder of the tragedy and serves as a poignant memorial to the victims. In recent years, there have been calls for greater recognition and commemoration of the sinking, both in Germany and internationally, as part of the broader effort to remember and honor the civilian victims of war.

The story of the Wilhelm Gustloff is a testament to the profound human cost of war and the enduring impact of maritime disasters on collective memory. It serves as a powerful reminder of the fragility of life and the importance of remembering the past to inform a more compassionate and just future. The legacy of the Wilhelm Gustloff continues to resonate, offering valuable lessons on the nature of conflict, the resilience of the human spirit, and the imperative of historical remembrance.

# Chapter 7: SS Eastland

The SS Eastland disaster is a tragic chapter in maritime history that continues to resonate over a century later. Occurring on July 24, 1915, in the Chicago River, this catastrophe led to the deaths of 844 passengers and crew, making it one of the deadliest maritime accidents in American history. The story of the SS Eastland is a complex narrative that intertwines industrial ambition, regulatory shortcomings, and the harsh realities of early 20th-century maritime travel. To fully understand the gravity of the disaster, one must delve into the history of the vessel, the circumstances surrounding the accident, and the profound impact it had on maritime safety regulations and the collective memory of Chicago and beyond.

The SS Eastland was a passenger steamer built in 1903 by the Jenks Ship Building Company of Port Huron, Michigan. Measuring 275 feet in length and weighing 1,961 gross tons, the Eastland was designed to operate on the Great Lakes, carrying passengers between major cities such as Chicago, Cleveland, and Detroit. The ship was part of a burgeoning fleet of vessels intended to cater to the growing demand for leisure travel among the urban working class. During this period, the Great Lakes were a major hub for both commerce and tourism, with numerous steamers plying their waters.

From its inception, the SS Eastland was plagued by stability issues. The ship was constructed with a relatively shallow draft, which made it prone to listing, particularly when loaded with passengers. This design flaw was evident from its early voyages, with several reports of the ship listing alarmingly under various conditions. Despite these issues, the Eastland continued to operate, often overloaded and with little regard for the potential safety hazards.

The disaster on July 24, 1915, was precipitated by a series of unfortunate events and decisions. On that fateful day, the Eastland was chartered by the Western Electric Company to transport employees and their families from Chicago to a company picnic in Michigan City, Indiana. This outing was a much-anticipated event, offering a rare opportunity for factory workers and their families to enjoy a day of leisure away from the rigors of industrial labor. Over 2,500 tickets had been sold for the excursion, and the docks were crowded with excited passengers.

As the passengers began boarding the Eastland in the early morning hours, several factors conspired to set the stage for disaster. The ship was docked at the Clark Street Bridge on the south bank of the Chicago River, a location that was bustling with activity. The weather was warm and clear, ideal for a day on the water. However, as more people crowded onto the vessel, the inherent stability issues of the Eastland began to manifest.

By the time the ship had taken on more than 2,500 passengers, it was sitting low in the water. The crew attempted to compensate for the listing by moving ballast water, but these efforts were insufficient. Around 7:30 a.m., the ship began to list sharply to port. Panic ensued as passengers felt the vessel tilt and water started pouring in through the portholes on the lower decks. Within minutes, the list became uncontrollable, and the Eastland capsized in the Chicago River, coming to rest on its side in just 20 feet of water, mere yards from the dock.

The rapid capsizing left those on board with little time to react. Many passengers were trapped below deck, unable to escape the sudden inundation of water. The upper decks became a chaotic scene as people were thrown into the river or clung desperately to the ship's structure. Rescue efforts were immediate but chaotic. Bystanders on the dock, many of whom were waiting to board other ships for the same excursion, watched in horror as the disaster unfolded. They, along with emergency responders and passing boats, rushed to aid the victims, pulling survivors from the water and cutting through the ship's hull to reach those trapped inside.

Despite the valiant efforts of rescuers, the death toll was staggering. A total of 844 lives were lost, including many women and children. The aftermath of the disaster saw the makeshift morgues set up along the Chicago River's banks and in nearby warehouses to accommodate the overwhelming number of bodies. The tragedy left a deep scar on the community, as many of the victims were from the nearby suburb of Cicero, where the Western Electric Company was a major employer. Families were devastated, and entire communities mourned the loss of loved ones.

The inquiry into the disaster revealed a series of alarming failures and oversights. Investigators quickly identified the ship's chronic stability issues as a primary cause of the accident. The Eastland's shallow draft and high center of gravity made it prone to capsizing, particularly when overloaded with passengers. Furthermore, the addition of lifeboats and other safety equipment, mandated by recent maritime regulations following the sinking of the RMS Titanic in 1912, had only exacerbated the vessel's instability. The irony of these safety measures contributing to the disaster was not lost on the public or the investigators.

The ship's operators were found to have repeatedly ignored warnings and complaints about the Eastland's safety. Testimonies from crew members and previous passengers described numerous incidents of the ship listing dangerously, even on calm days with moderate loads. Despite these red flags, the ship had been allowed to continue operating without significant modifications or restrictions. The investigation also highlighted broader systemic issues within the maritime industry, including lax regulatory oversight and the prioritization of profit over safety.

In the wake of the Eastland disaster, there was a widespread public outcry for accountability and reform. The ship's owners, the St. Joseph-Chicago Steamship Company, faced legal action and intense scrutiny. While some individuals within the company were charged with negligence, the complexities of the legal system and the limited regulations of the time meant that few were held fully accountable for the tragedy. The disaster did, however, prompt significant changes in maritime safety regulations. New laws were enacted to ensure stricter inspections and stability requirements for passenger vessels, aiming to prevent similar catastrophes in the future.

The legacy of the Eastland disaster is profound, both in terms of its immediate impact and its long-term influence on maritime safety. The event is remembered not only for the staggering loss of life but also for the lessons it imparted about the importance of safety and accountability in the transportation industry. Over the years, the story of the Eastland has been commemorated through memorials, historical markers, and educational initiatives, ensuring that the victims are not forgotten and that the lessons of the disaster continue to resonate.

In the decades following the disaster, the memory of the Eastland has been kept alive by the descendants of the victims and by historians dedicated to preserving this chapter of Chicago's history. The site of the disaster, near the Clark Street Bridge, remains a place of somber reflection, marked by a plaque that honors the victims and serves as a reminder of the human cost of complacency and oversight. The Eastland Disaster Historical Society, established by descendants of the victims, has worked tirelessly to educate the public about the tragedy, organizing events, lectures, and exhibitions to keep the story alive.

The Eastland disaster also holds a significant place in the broader narrative of American labor history. The victims were predominantly working-class individuals, many of whom had come to Chicago seeking better opportunities and a chance to escape the hardships of their homelands. Their tragic deaths underscored the precariousness of life for many working people in the early 20th century and highlighted the need for greater protections and rights for laborers. The disaster's impact on the community of Cicero and the Western Electric

Company workers illustrated the profound interconnectedness of industrial labor, community life, and personal tragedy.

The story of the SS Eastland is a poignant reminder of the fragility of human life and the critical importance of vigilance, safety, and compassion in all endeavors. It is a narrative that underscores the potential for disaster when profit and expedience are placed above the welfare of individuals and communities. The lessons learned from the Eastland continue to inform contemporary practices in maritime safety and regulation, serving as a testament to the enduring significance of this tragic event. Through remembrance and reflection, the legacy of the Eastland disaster endures, reminding us of the need for constant vigilance in the face of human and technological fallibility.

# Chapter 8: Empress of Ireland

The Empress of Ireland, a Canadian Pacific Steamship, holds a tragic place in maritime history as one of the deadliest shipwrecks of the 20th century. The disaster, which occurred on May 29, 1914, in the St. Lawrence River near Rimouski, Quebec, resulted in the loss of 1,012 lives. Despite its devastating impact, the story of the Empress of Ireland is often overshadowed by the sinking of the Titanic, which happened two years earlier. However, the Empress of Ireland's story is equally poignant, marked by a sequence of tragic events that culminated in a catastrophic collision, and it remains a significant chapter in the annals of maritime disasters.

The Empress of Ireland was launched on January 27, 1906, from the Fairfield Shipbuilding and Engineering Company in Govan, Scotland. It was one of two ships ordered by the Canadian Pacific Railway to serve the transatlantic route between Liverpool, England, and Quebec City, Canada. The ship was designed to be both luxurious and fast, catering to the growing demand for transatlantic travel among both immigrants seeking new opportunities in North America and tourists desiring a comfortable passage. With a length of 570 feet and a gross tonnage of 14,191, the Empress of Ireland was a sizable vessel, capable of carrying over 1,500 passengers along with a substantial crew.

The ship's design included all the amenities expected of a first-class ocean liner of the time, including elegant dining rooms, comfortable staterooms, and spacious promenades. The Empress of Ireland was divided into three classes, with first class offering the highest level of luxury, followed by second class and third class, which primarily accommodated immigrants. The ship's maiden voyage was on June 29, 1906, and it quickly gained a reputation for reliability and comfort, making it a popular choice for transatlantic travelers.

The Empress of Ireland's fateful voyage began on May 28, 1914, when it departed from Quebec City bound for Liverpool. On board were 1,477 people, including 420 crew members. The passengers represented a cross-section of society, from affluent tourists to working-class immigrants and members of the Salvation Army traveling to an international congress in London. The ship's captain, Henry George Kendall, was an experienced mariner who had taken command of the Empress of Ireland just three months earlier. The ship's departure was uneventful, and it proceeded down the St. Lawrence River toward the open sea.

However, as the ship approached the mouth of the St. Lawrence River in the early hours of May 29, a thick fog began to envelop the area, reducing visibility to almost zero. The Empress of Ireland was navigating through this treacherous stretch of water, which was notorious for its unpredictable weather and strong currents. At approximately 1:55 a.m., while navigating through the fog, the Empress of Ireland encountered the Norwegian collier SS Storstad. The Storstad, under the command of Captain Thomas Andersen, was carrying a cargo of coal from Sydney, Nova Scotia, to Rouen, France.

The exact circumstances of the collision remain a matter of historical debate, but it is generally agreed that both ships were navigating cautiously due to the fog. The Empress of Ireland had sounded its foghorn, and Captain Kendall had ordered the ship to slow down and maintain a steady course. Meanwhile, the Storstad was also proceeding slowly and attempting to navigate through the dense fog. The two ships were on a collision course, but due to the limited visibility, they did not spot each other until it was too late to take effective evasive action.

At around 2:00 a.m., the Storstad's bow collided with the starboard side of the Empress of Ireland, striking it amidships and creating a massive gash in the hull. The impact was catastrophic, causing immediate and severe flooding of the lower decks. The Empress of Ireland began to list heavily to starboard as water poured into the ship's compartments. Within minutes, the list became so severe that it was impossible to launch the lifeboats on the starboard side. The passengers and crew were thrown into a state of panic as they scrambled to escape the rapidly sinking ship.

The ship's distress signals were sent out, but the rapid flooding and list made an orderly evacuation impossible. Many of the passengers were trapped in their cabins or unable to reach the upper decks in time. The cold waters of the St. Lawrence River added to the peril, as those who managed to escape the ship faced the immediate threat of hypothermia. The ship sank so quickly that within 14 minutes of the collision, the Empress of Ireland had disappeared beneath the waves, taking over 1,000 people with it.

The rescue efforts that followed were hampered by the darkness and the dense fog. Nearby ships, including the Lady Evelyn and the Eureka, responded to the distress signals and arrived at the scene to rescue survivors. However, the speed of the sinking and the chaotic conditions made it difficult to save many lives. Of the 1,477 people on board, only 465 survived. The majority of the victims were third-class passengers, who had the least time and opportunity to escape the lower decks. The crew also suffered significant losses, with many going down with the ship as they attempted to help passengers.

The aftermath of the Empress of Ireland disaster was marked by shock and mourning on both sides of the Atlantic. The loss of so many lives, including entire families and groups such as the Salvation Army delegation, had a profound impact on communities and organizations. In Canada, the disaster was a national tragedy, and in the United Kingdom, it was seen as another in a series of devastating maritime losses, coming just two years after the Titanic and less than a year after the sinking of the RMS Lusitania by a German U-boat.

The official inquiry into the disaster sought to determine the causes and assign responsibility for the collision. The inquiry, held in Quebec City, lasted for several weeks and involved testimonies from surviving crew members, passengers, and maritime experts. The inquiry concluded that both ships bore some responsibility for the collision, but it placed a greater share of the blame on the captain of the Storstad for not taking adequate measures to avoid the collision. However, the captain of the Storstad and its owners contested this finding, arguing that the Empress of Ireland had made an unexpected course change that brought the two ships into a collision course.

The inquiry also highlighted the broader issues of maritime safety and the challenges of navigating through dense fog in busy shipping lanes. It called for improved regulations and better safety measures to prevent similar disasters in the future. Among the recommendations were enhanced training for ship captains and crews, better communication protocols between ships, and stricter enforcement of safety standards for passenger vessels.

In the years following the disaster, the wreck of the Empress of Ireland was explored by divers and became a focal point for salvage operations. Numerous artifacts were recovered from the wreck, including personal belongings of the passengers, items from the ship's cargo, and parts of the ship itself. These artifacts have been displayed in museums and exhibitions, providing a tangible link to the tragedy and serving as a reminder of the lives lost.

The Empress of Ireland disaster also had a lasting impact on the shipping industry and maritime regulations. It underscored the need for continuous improvement in safety standards and practices, particularly for passenger vessels. The lessons learned from the disaster contributed to the development of more stringent safety regulations and the establishment of better safety protocols for ship navigation, particularly in challenging conditions such as fog.

The memory of the Empress of Ireland disaster has been kept alive through commemorations, memorials, and historical research. In Rimouski, near the site of the sinking, a museum dedicated to the Empress of Ireland was established to honor the victims and educate the public about the disaster. The museum features exhibits on the ship's history, the events of the night of the sinking, and the subsequent rescue efforts and investigations. It also displays artifacts recovered from the wreck, offering a poignant connection to the lives of those who perished.

The Empress of Ireland disaster remains an important part of Canadian and maritime history, serving as a reminder of the dangers of sea travel and the need for ongoing vigilance in ensuring the safety of those who venture onto the water. It also stands as a testament to the resilience of the human spirit in the face of tragedy, as survivors and their descendants have worked to preserve the memory of the disaster and honor the legacy of those who were lost. The story of the Empress of Ireland continues to resonate with people today, reflecting the enduring significance of this tragic event in the broader context of maritime history.

# Chapter 9: SS Edmund Fitzgerald

The SS Edmund Fitzgerald was a massive American Great Lakes freighter that became an icon of maritime history due to its tragic sinking in Lake Superior on November 10, 1975. This vessel, affectionately nicknamed the "Mighty Fitz," was launched on June 7, 1958, and was the largest ship on the Great Lakes at the time of her launch. Built by the Great Lakes Engineering Works in River Rouge, Michigan, the Fitzgerald was a technological marvel of her time, measuring 729 feet in length, 75 feet in width, and 39 feet in depth. She was capable of carrying 26,600 tons of cargo, primarily iron ore, and was operated by the Northwestern Mutual Life Insurance Company, which had invested heavily in the construction of this mighty vessel.

The Fitzgerald's final voyage began on the afternoon of November 9, 1975, from Superior, Wisconsin, loaded with 26,116 tons of taconite pellets bound for a steel mill near Detroit, Michigan. Captain Ernest M. McSorley, a seasoned mariner with decades of experience, commanded the ship. The vessel was accompanied by another ship, the SS Arthur M. Anderson, which would play a crucial role in the events that unfolded. The weather forecast predicted a major storm, but such storms were not uncommon in November on the Great Lakes, often referred to as "The Gales of November."

As the ships made their way across Lake Superior, the weather rapidly deteriorated. By the evening of November 9, the National Weather Service had upgraded the storm warning to an all-out gale, with winds exceeding 50 knots and waves reaching up to 35 feet. Despite these harsh conditions, both ships continued their journey, maintaining radio contact. By the next day, November 10, the storm had intensified further. The Fitzgerald reported some damage, including a fence rail down and two vents lost or damaged. However, McSorley did not seem overly concerned at this point.

By early afternoon, the situation had worsened. McSorley radioed the Anderson to report that the Fitzgerald was taking on water and had lost two radar systems, making navigation extremely challenging in the storm's fury. Despite these setbacks, McSorley assured that they were "holding their own." The last communication from the Fitzgerald came at approximately 7:10 p.m. when McSorley told the Anderson, "We are holding our own." Just a few minutes later, the Fitzgerald disappeared from the radar screen of the Anderson, which was trailing about 10 miles behind.

The crew of the Anderson tried desperately to establish radio contact with the Fitzgerald but received no response. A search was initiated, but the night and the storm's intensity made the effort extraordinarily difficult. The Coast Guard and other vessels joined the search at first light, but no survivors were found. All 29 crew members aboard the Edmund Fitzgerald perished. The ship's remains were later found resting in two large pieces on the lake bed, at a depth of about 530 feet.

The sinking of the Edmund Fitzgerald remains one of the greatest maritime mysteries and tragedies in the history of the Great Lakes. Numerous theories have been proposed to explain what happened that fateful night. Some suggest that the ship may have been overwhelmed by the massive waves, particularly the so-called "three sisters" – a series of three consecutive, unusually large waves. Another theory posits that the ship may have struck a shoal or an underwater obstruction, compromising its hull integrity. Some experts believe that structural failure could have played a role, possibly exacerbated by the heavy load and the stress of the storm. The exact cause of the sinking remains unknown, and it is likely that a combination of factors contributed to the disaster.

The loss of the Edmund Fitzgerald had a profound impact on maritime practices and safety regulations on the Great Lakes. In the aftermath of the tragedy, the U.S. Coast Guard conducted a thorough investigation and implemented several safety improvements, including better weather forecasting, mandatory survival suits, and increased inspections of vessels. The wreck of the Fitzgerald also captured the public's imagination, immortalized by Gordon Lightfoot's haunting ballad "The Wreck of the Edmund Fitzgerald," which became a hit in 1976 and remains a poignant tribute to the lost crew.

To this day, the Edmund Fitzgerald is remembered with solemnity and respect. Annual memorial services are held at the Mariners' Church in Detroit, known as the "Church of the Maritime Sailors' Cathedral," where the ship's bell is tolled 29 times, once for each lost sailor. The Great Lakes Shipwreck Museum at Whitefish Point, Michigan, also honors the memory of the Fitzgerald's crew, displaying the ship's recovered bell and other artifacts. The legend of the Edmund Fitzgerald endures as a powerful reminder of the dangers of maritime navigation and the enduring mystery of what happened on that stormy November night in 1975.

# Chapter 10: MV Doña Paz

The MV Doña Paz was a Philippine-registered passenger ferry that became infamous due to the tragic maritime disaster that occurred on December 20, 1987. Often referred to as Asia's Titanic, the incident is considered the deadliest peacetime maritime disaster in history, with an estimated death toll exceeding 4,300 people. The MV Doña Paz was originally built in Japan in 1963 and named Himeyuri Maru. It was later sold to Sulpicio Lines, a Filipino company, and renamed Doña Paz in 1975. The ferry was primarily used for inter-island travel in the Philippines, connecting the islands of Leyte and Manila.

On the evening of December 20, 1987, the MV Doña Paz departed from Tacloban City on Leyte Island, bound for Manila. The ferry was reportedly overcrowded, carrying more passengers than its official capacity of 1,518. Eyewitness accounts and subsequent investigations suggested that there were many more people aboard, including a significant number of unlisted passengers. The ship was operating under less-than-ideal conditions, with allegations that some of the life jackets and other safety equipment were either inadequate or missing.

As the ferry made its way through the Tablas Strait, an area known for its heavy maritime traffic, disaster struck. At approximately 10:30 PM, the MV Doña Paz collided with the MT Vector, an oil tanker carrying a substantial cargo of petroleum products, including gasoline and kerosene. The collision caused a massive explosion on the Vector, which quickly spread to the Doña Paz. The ensuing fire engulfed both vessels in a matter of minutes. The force of the explosion and the rapidly spreading flames left passengers and crew with little time to react. Many passengers were asleep at the time of the collision and were caught unaware by the sudden chaos. The panic was exacerbated by the apparent lack of preparedness and insufficient safety measures aboard the ferry. There were reports that many life jackets were inaccessible or unusable, and the lifeboats were not effectively deployed.

The fire from the MT Vector's petroleum cargo created a catastrophic situation. The burning oil spread on the surface of the water, creating a deadly inferno that trapped many passengers. Those who jumped into the sea faced the grim prospect of being caught in the flames or succumbing to the oil-covered, toxic waters. The crew of the Doña Paz was reportedly ill-prepared for such an emergency, with many unable to provide adequate assistance or direction to the panicking passengers.

Rescue operations were hampered by the remoteness of the disaster site and the sheer scale of the devastation. The Philippine Coast Guard and other vessels in the vicinity responded, but by the time they arrived, the Doña Paz had already sunk. Most of the survivors were picked up from the water by passing ships, notably the MV Don Claudio, which managed to rescue a few survivors. In the end, only 24 people from the MV Doña Paz and two crew members from the MT Vector were rescued alive. The official death toll was recorded at 1,749, but estimates suggest that the actual number of victims could be as high as 4,386, including unregistered passengers and crew.

In the aftermath of the disaster, the Philippine government launched an investigation to determine the cause and assign responsibility. The inquiry revealed several alarming details about the operation of both vessels. The MV Doña Paz was found to be grossly overburdened and inadequately equipped with safety measures. There were also questions about the competency and preparedness of the crew. The MT Vector, on the other hand, was discovered to be operating without a proper license, and its crew was found to be inadequately trained for the handling of such a hazardous cargo. The investigation concluded that the collision was due to human error and negligence on both sides. The MT Vector's crew was found to be primarily at fault for the collision, as the tanker had veered off course and into the path of the ferry. The Doña Paz's crew was also criticized for their failure to take appropriate evasive action and their poor handling of the emergency situation.

The disaster had a profound impact on maritime regulations and practices in the Philippines and beyond. It exposed severe deficiencies in safety standards and the enforcement of maritime laws. In response, the Philippine government implemented stricter regulations for passenger ferries, including mandatory safety equipment checks, proper documentation of passengers, and more rigorous training for crew members. Despite these changes, the memory of the MV Doña Paz disaster continues to haunt the Philippine maritime industry. It serves as a stark reminder of the potentially catastrophic consequences of negligence and poor safety practices at sea. The tragedy is commemorated annually, and the stories of the victims and survivors are remembered in various memorials and ceremonies.

The MV Doña Paz disaster remains one of the most harrowing maritime tragedies in history. It is a poignant example of how a combination of human error, inadequate safety measures, and regulatory failures can lead to unimaginable loss. The disaster not only brought about significant changes in maritime safety regulations but also left an indelible mark on the collective memory of the Philippines and the global maritime community. The lessons learned from this tragic event continue to resonate, underscoring the importance of vigilance, preparedness, and strict adherence to safety protocols in preventing similar catastrophes in the future.

# **Chapter 11: Costa Concordia**

The Costa Concordia was a luxury cruise ship operated by Costa Crociere, a subsidiary of Carnival Corporation. It became widely known for its dramatic and tragic grounding and subsequent sinking on January 13, 2012, off the coast of Isola del Giglio, Tuscany, Italy. The disaster claimed the lives of 32 people, with 64 more injured, and left an indelible mark on maritime history and safety protocols.

The Costa Concordia, built by the Fincantieri Sestri Ponente shipyard in Italy, was launched in 2005. It was one of the largest cruise ships in the world at the time, measuring 952 feet in length, 116 feet in width, and having a gross tonnage of 114,137 tons. The ship was designed to carry up to 3,780 passengers and 1,100 crew members, offering luxurious amenities such as multiple restaurants, bars, a theater, spa, and swimming pools. On January 13, 2012, the Costa Concordia departed from the port of Civitavecchia, near Rome, for a seven-day Mediterranean cruise. The ship was under the command of Captain Francesco Schettino, an experienced mariner with over 30 years at sea.

As the ship sailed along the western coast of Italy, Captain Schettino decided to perform a "salute" maneuver, bringing the ship close to the island of Giglio. This practice, known as "tourist navigation," was intended to give passengers a spectacular view of the island and had been done on previous occasions. However, this time, the maneuver went disastrously wrong. At approximately 9:45 PM local time, the Costa Concordia struck a rock formation known as Le Scole, which was not on the ship's planned route and dangerously close to the shoreline. The impact caused a 174-foot gash on the port side of the hull, resulting in the flooding of multiple compartments, including the engine room, and leading to a loss of power.

The immediate aftermath of the collision was marked by confusion and panic. Passengers reported feeling a severe jolt, followed by a blackout and a loud scraping noise as the ship hit the rocks. Despite the severity of the situation, the crew initially downplayed the incident, with announcements suggesting a minor electrical fault. It was not until the ship began to list heavily to starboard that the true extent of the damage became apparent. As the ship started to tilt, passengers and crew faced chaotic conditions. Evacuation orders were delayed, and the lifeboat deployment was hindered by the increasing list of the ship. The crew's lack of preparedness for such an emergency was evident, leading to further confusion and delays in the evacuation process. Passengers recounted scenes of panic as they tried to navigate darkened corridors and flooded stairwells to reach the lifeboat stations.

The evacuation was hampered by the fact that many lifeboats could not be launched due to the ship's angle. Some passengers and crew were forced to jump into the cold, dark waters and swim to safety. Local residents of Giglio, as well as nearby boats, responded to the distress signals and assisted in the rescue efforts. The Italian Coast Guard, along with other rescue agencies, launched a major operation to evacuate the passengers and crew. Despite these efforts, 32 people lost their lives in the disaster, including two crew members and 30 passengers. The bodies of two victims were not recovered until years later, during the salvage operations.

In the days following the disaster, Captain Francesco Schettino became a central figure of controversy and scrutiny. He was accused of abandoning ship while hundreds of passengers were still on board, a serious breach of maritime tradition and duty. Schettino defended his actions by claiming that he had accidentally fallen into a lifeboat and insisted that he coordinated the evacuation from the shore. However, recorded conversations between Schettino and the Italian Coast Guard revealed that he had indeed left the ship prematurely and failed to take decisive action during the critical moments of the disaster.

The Costa Concordia disaster triggered a massive international response and led to widespread media coverage. The Italian government, maritime authorities, and Costa Crociere launched investigations into the causes and handling of the incident. These inquiries revealed a series of failures, including human error, poor judgment, and inadequate safety measures. Captain Schettino was found to have deviated from the planned route without authorization and to have navigated the ship dangerously close to shore. Additionally, the crew's lack of training and the insufficient emergency preparedness onboard were cited as contributing factors to the high casualty rate.

Legal proceedings against Captain Schettino and other crew members ensued. In 2015, Schettino was convicted of multiple charges, including manslaughter, causing a maritime disaster, and abandoning ship. He was sentenced to 16 years in prison. Costa Crociere faced significant legal and financial repercussions, including lawsuits from survivors and the families of the victims. The company reached settlements with many of the affected parties and agreed to pay fines and compensation.

The wreck of the Costa Concordia remained partially submerged off the coast of Giglio for more than two years, becoming a stark reminder of the disaster. Salvage operations, led by the Italian-American consortium Titan-Micoperi, were unprecedented in scale and complexity. The operation involved stabilizing the wreck, refloating the ship using a technique known as parbuckling, and towing it to the port of Genoa for dismantling and recycling. The successful completion of the salvage operation in July 2014 was hailed as a remarkable engineering feat.

The Costa Concordia disaster had far-reaching implications for the cruise industry and maritime safety regulations. The International Maritime Organization (IMO) and other regulatory bodies introduced stricter safety standards and emergency procedures for passenger ships. These measures included mandatory lifeboat drills before departure, improved crew training, and more rigorous inspections of safety equipment. The disaster also prompted a re-evaluation of the practice of tourist navigation and the proximity of cruise routes to shorelines.

Despite the regulatory changes, the legacy of the Costa Concordia disaster endures as a stark reminder of the potential dangers of complacency and human error in maritime operations. The disaster highlighted the importance of adherence to safety protocols, the need for effective emergency preparedness, and the critical role of leadership and decision-making in crisis situations. The memory of the victims and the lessons learned from the tragedy continue to influence the maritime industry and serve as a cautionary tale for future generations.

# Chapter 12: HMS Victoria

HMS Victoria was a British battleship whose sinking on June 22, 1893, stands as one of the most significant peacetime naval disasters in the history of the Royal Navy. The incident not only resulted in the loss of the ship and over 350 lives but also highlighted critical issues in naval tactics, ship design, and command decisions.

Launched in 1887, HMS Victoria was the lead ship of the Victoria-class battleships, designed during an era of rapid naval innovation. The ship was constructed at the Elswick shipyard of Armstrong Whitworth, an esteemed British engineering company. Victoria was notable for her unique design, featuring a powerful ram bow, which was intended for offensive naval maneuvers. This design was controversial and became a central factor in her eventual demise. Victoria was 340 feet long, with a beam of 70 feet and a displacement of 10,470 tons. She was heavily armed, carrying two 16.25-inch guns in a single turret forward and a secondary armament of twelve 6-inch guns. The ship's armor protection was formidable for its time, with a belt of up to 18 inches of compound armor. She was powered by twin screws driven by coal-fired steam engines, capable of reaching speeds of up to 17 knots.

In the years leading up to the disaster, HMS Victoria served as the flagship of the Mediterranean Fleet, one of the most prestigious commands in the Royal Navy. The fleet was under the command of Vice-Admiral Sir George Tryon, a distinguished and experienced officer known for his innovative and sometimes controversial ideas about naval tactics and fleet maneuvering. On June 22, 1893, the Mediterranean Fleet was conducting maneuvers off the coast of Tripoli, Lebanon. The exercises involved complex formations and were intended to test the fleet's readiness and the effectiveness of Tryon's new tactical ideas. Tryon ordered the fleet to perform a maneuver that required two parallel columns of ships to turn inward toward each other and reverse their direction. This maneuver, while theoretically sound, required precise timing and coordination to avoid collision.

As the ships began the turn, it became apparent that the columns were too close to each other to safely execute the maneuver. Captain Maurice Bourke of HMS Camperdown, which was leading the other column, expressed his concerns but was overruled by Tryon. The fleet proceeded with the maneuver, and disaster struck when HMS Victoria and HMS Camperdown collided. The ram bow of Camperdown tore into Victoria's starboard side, causing catastrophic damage. The collision created a massive hole in Victoria's hull, and within minutes, the ship began to list heavily to starboard. Despite efforts to save the ship, it was clear that she was sinking rapidly. The order to abandon ship was given, but the process was chaotic due to the severe list and the short amount of time available.

As Victoria continued to heel over, she eventually capsized and sank bow-first, her stern lifting high into the air before disappearing beneath the waves. The ship sank in just 13 minutes, trapping many men inside. Of the approximately 600 crew members on board, 358 perished, including Vice-Admiral Tryon. The loss of life was significant, and many of the survivors were left in shock and disbelief at the sudden and tragic turn of events.

The sinking of HMS Victoria sent shockwaves through the Royal Navy and the wider public. An inquiry was immediately convened to investigate the circumstances surrounding the disaster. The inquiry focused on several key issues, including the design of the ship, the tactics employed during the maneuver, and the decisions made by Vice-Admiral Tryon. One of the primary points of contention was Tryon's insistence on executing a maneuver that required precise spacing and timing. Critics argued that the maneuver was unnecessarily risky and that Tryon should have heeded the concerns of his subordinates. The inquiry also examined the role of the ship's design in the disaster. The ram bow, intended as an offensive weapon, had instead contributed to the ship's rapid sinking. The placement of the main turret forward also affected the ship's stability and may have exacerbated the listing when the hull was breached.

Vice-Admiral Tryon's actions were scrutinized extensively. Known for his authoritarian leadership style, Tryon was respected but also feared within the fleet. His decision to proceed with the maneuver despite the apparent risks was ultimately deemed a grave error in judgment. The inquiry concluded that Tryon had overestimated the capabilities of his ships and had failed to adequately consider the potential consequences of his orders. The sinking of HMS Victoria had far-reaching implications for naval tactics and ship design. The disaster prompted a reevaluation of the use of ram bows and highlighted the need for more robust safety protocols during fleet maneuvers. It also underscored the importance of clear communication and the need for commanders to consider the input of their subordinates when making critical decisions.

In the aftermath of the disaster, changes were made to improve the safety and effectiveness of fleet operations. The Royal Navy introduced new training programs to ensure that officers were better prepared to handle complex maneuvers. Additionally, there was a greater emphasis on the importance of maintaining adequate spacing between ships during exercises to prevent collisions. The legacy of HMS Victoria also influenced the design of future battleships. Naval architects became more cautious about incorporating ram bows into new designs, and there was an increased focus on improving the overall stability and survivability of warships. The lessons learned from the sinking contributed to the development of more advanced and safer naval vessels in the years that followed.

Despite the tragic outcome, the story of HMS Victoria remains a poignant reminder of the inherent risks of naval warfare and the critical importance of sound leadership and decision-making. The disaster serves as a case study in the potential consequences of human error and the need for continuous improvement in naval tactics and technology. The wreck of HMS Victoria was discovered in 2004 by a team of Lebanese and British divers, resting on the seabed at a depth of around 150 meters. The discovery of the wreck provided valuable insights into the final moments of the ship and offered a somber opportunity to reflect on the lives lost in the disaster. Artifacts recovered from the site have been preserved and are displayed in various naval museums, serving as a tangible connection to the past and a reminder of the sacrifices made by those who serve at sea.

# Chapter 13: SS Sultana

The SS Sultana was a Mississippi River side-wheel steamboat that became infamous for one of the worst maritime disasters in American history. The catastrophic explosion and sinking of the SS Sultana on April 27, 1865, resulted in the deaths of an estimated 1,800 passengers, most of whom were recently released Union soldiers returning home after the end of the American Civil War. This tragedy stands as a poignant and often overlooked chapter in the annals of American history.

The SS Sultana was built in 1863 in Cincinnati, Ohio, and was intended for transporting cotton and passengers between St. Louis, Missouri, and New Orleans, Louisiana. The steamboat measured 260 feet in length and 42 feet in width and was designed to carry a maximum of 376 passengers. She was powered by four tubular boilers, which were prone to wear and tear but were a common design for riverboats of that era. The Sultana was a luxurious vessel by the standards of the time, offering comfortable accommodations and amenities for its passengers.

In the spring of 1865, the Civil War had just ended, and thousands of Union soldiers who had been held in Confederate prison camps were being released and transported back to their homes. The U.S. government contracted various riverboats to carry these men northward, providing an opportunity for boat operators to profit from the surge in demand. Among these operators was Captain J. Cass Mason, the master of the SS Sultana. Despite concerns about the boat's condition and the capacity limits, Mason was eager to maximize profits by taking on as many passengers as possible.

The Sultana departed from New Orleans on April 21, 1865, heading north to Cairo, Illinois. Along the way, she stopped at Vicksburg, Mississippi, where the majority of the passengers, former Union prisoners of war, boarded the vessel. These men had endured horrific conditions in prison camps such as Andersonville and Cahaba and were in a weakened state, both physically and emotionally. The Sultana was grossly overloaded, with estimates suggesting that more than 2,300 people were crammed onto a boat designed for fewer than 400. This overloading was exacerbated by a bribe paid to an Army officer to ensure that the Sultana would carry the bulk of the soldiers, further pushing her capacity far beyond safe limits.

Compounding the danger was the condition of the Sultana's boilers. Just a few days before the ill-fated voyage, one of the boilers had developed a leak and was hastily patched rather than properly repaired. The patch was a temporary fix, inadequate for the strain that would be placed on the boilers during the journey upstream against the strong current of the Mississippi River. Despite the known risks, Captain Mason pressed on, driven by the financial incentives and the pressure to deliver his human cargo.

In the early hours of April 27, 1865, as the Sultana navigated the river near Memphis, Tennessee, disaster struck. At around 2:00 AM, one of the overburdened boilers exploded, triggering a chain reaction that caused the remaining boilers to burst. The explosions were catastrophic, ripping through the center of the ship and instantly killing hundreds of passengers and crew. The blast was so powerful that it shattered the upper decks, flinging many passengers into the frigid river waters below.

In the chaotic moments following the explosion, the Sultana quickly became an inferno. Fire spread rapidly through the wreckage, fueled by the wooden superstructure of the ship. Many of those who survived the initial explosion were trapped in the burning wreckage, while others faced the desperate choice of jumping into the river or being consumed by the flames. The icy waters of the Mississippi presented a deadly challenge for the exhausted and weakened soldiers, many of whom were unable to swim.

Rescue efforts were hampered by the darkness and the swift current of the river. Nearby boats, including the USS Tyler, a Union gunboat, and various civilian vessels, responded to the scene and managed to pull some survivors from the water. Local residents also joined the rescue efforts, using whatever means they had to save those struggling in the river. Despite these heroic efforts, the vast majority of those on board perished in the disaster.

The aftermath of the SS Sultana tragedy was marked by confusion, grief, and a search for answers. The official death toll was difficult to determine due to the chaotic boarding process and the incomplete passenger lists. Estimates of the number of deaths range from 1,168 to as high as 1,800, making it the deadliest maritime disaster in U.S. history. The tragedy was overshadowed by other significant events of the time, including the assassination of President Abraham Lincoln and the end of the Civil War, which contributed to the relative obscurity of the Sultana disaster in the annals of American history.

An investigation was launched to determine the cause of the explosion and assign responsibility. The inquiry revealed a series of failures and oversights, including the overloaded condition of the ship, the inadequate repairs to the boiler, and the negligence of Captain Mason and other officials involved in the operation. Despite the findings, no one was held criminally accountable for the disaster, and many of the key figures involved escaped significant repercussions.

The legacy of the SS Sultana disaster is a sobering reminder of the consequences of greed, negligence, and the disregard for human life. The tragedy prompted some changes in steamboat safety regulations, but it also highlighted the vulnerabilities and limitations of the technology and practices of the time. The memory of the disaster has been kept alive through the efforts of historians, descendants of the victims, and organizations dedicated to preserving the history of the event.

In recent years, renewed interest in the Sultana disaster has led to further research and exploration. In 1982, the wreckage of the SS Sultana was discovered buried in a field near Marion, Arkansas, several miles from the current course of the Mississippi River. This discovery provided valuable insights into the final moments of the ship and helped to bring the story of the Sultana to a wider audience. Efforts to commemorate the victims and educate the public about the disaster continue, with museums, documentaries, and memorials dedicated to preserving the legacy of the SS Sultana and those who perished in the tragedy.

The SS Sultana disaster remains a poignant chapter in American history, illustrating the devastating impact of human error and the often-overlooked stories of those who suffered in its wake. It serves as a testament to the resilience of the survivors and the enduring importance of remembering and learning from the past.

# Chapter 14: MS Estonia

The MS Estonia disaster, which occurred on the night of September 28, 1994, is one of the most tragic and significant maritime disasters in European history, particularly in the post-World War II era. The ship's sinking in the Baltic Sea resulted in the loss of 852 lives out of the 989 people on board, making it one of the deadliest peacetime maritime disasters of the 20th century. The tragedy not only highlighted severe flaws in maritime safety practices but also led to significant changes in international maritime regulations.

The MS Estonia was a cruise ferry built in 1980 at the German shipyard Meyer Werft in Papenburg. Initially named Viking Sally, she was designed for the Finnish company Viking Line. The ship measured 510 feet in length and 79 feet in width, with a gross tonnage of 15,566 tons. She could accommodate up to 2,000 passengers and had a cargo capacity for 460 cars. The ferry featured a distinctive bow visor, a large front door that could be raised to allow vehicles to enter and exit the cargo hold. This bow visor design would later become a critical point of focus in the investigation of the disaster.

The Estonia changed hands several times before being acquired by Estline Marine Company and renamed MS Estonia in 1993. She was primarily used for ferrying passengers and cargo between Tallinn, Estonia, and Stockholm, Sweden. The route was popular among travelers and business people, providing a vital connection between the two countries. On the evening of September 27, 1994, the MS Estonia departed from Tallinn on what should have been a routine overnight voyage to Stockholm. The ship was carrying 989 people, including passengers and crew. The weather conditions at the time of departure were not ideal, with reports of strong winds and rough seas in the Baltic Sea. However, such conditions were not uncommon for the region, and the crew did not consider them unusually dangerous.

As the night progressed, the weather worsened, with gale-force winds and waves reaching heights of up to 20 feet. At around 1:00 AM on September 28, the ship was in the middle of the Baltic Sea, near the Finnish island of Utö. At this point, passengers and crew members began to notice strange noises coming from the bow area. These noises were later identified as the sounds of the bow visor being torn off by the force of the waves. The bow visor's failure was catastrophic. It caused the watertight ramp behind it to open, allowing large amounts of water to flood the car deck. The sudden influx of water severely compromised the ship's stability. The Estonia quickly developed a heavy list to starboard, making it increasingly difficult for the crew and passengers to move around.

The situation deteriorated rapidly. Within minutes, the list became so severe that lifeboats and life rafts on the port side became unusable. The crew attempted to send out distress signals, but the ship's severe tilt and the chaos on board made it challenging to maintain communication. Despite the efforts of the crew, the ship continued to capsize and sink. Many passengers were trapped inside the ship as it listed further and ultimately capsized. The freezing water temperature and the rough sea conditions made survival difficult even for those who managed to abandon ship. Some lifeboats were successfully launched, but they quickly became overcrowded, and many people were left clinging to debris in the water.

The distress signals sent by the MS Estonia were picked up by the maritime rescue coordination centers in Sweden and Finland. A massive search and rescue operation was launched, involving helicopters, ships, and other rescue assets from several countries. The first rescuers arrived at the scene within hours, but by then, the majority of the survivors were already in the water. The rescue efforts were hampered by the severe weather conditions, making it difficult to locate and retrieve survivors. In total, 137 people were rescued alive, but 852 lives were lost, including passengers and crew from various countries.

The immediate aftermath of the disaster was marked by shock and grief, particularly in Estonia, Sweden, and Finland, which bore the brunt of the losses.

In the wake of the sinking, several investigations were launched to determine the causes of the disaster and to identify measures to prevent similar incidents in the future. The most significant of these was conducted by the Joint Accident Investigation Commission (JAIC), which included representatives from Estonia, Finland, and Sweden. The commission's final report, published in 1997, identified the failure of the bow visor and the subsequent flooding of the car deck as the primary causes of the sinking. The report concluded that the locks securing the bow visor were inadequate to withstand the forces of the storm, leading to its failure. Once the bow visor was torn off, the unprotected car deck allowed water to flood in, quickly destabilizing the ship.

The JAIC report also highlighted several contributory factors, including design flaws in the bow visor and car deck, as well as issues with the crew's response to the emergency. The investigation revealed that the crew had not been adequately trained to deal with such a catastrophic failure, and the evacuation procedures were insufficient given the severity of the situation. In addition to the official investigations, there were numerous independent inquiries and theories about the disaster. Some of these alternative theories suggested that the Estonia might have been carrying illegal military cargo, or that the ship had been damaged by an explosion. However, these theories were not supported by conclusive evidence and remain speculative.

The sinking of the MS Estonia led to significant changes in international maritime safety regulations. The International Maritime Organization (IMO) introduced stricter standards for the design and construction of passenger ships, particularly regarding the securing and watertight integrity of bow visors and other critical components. The disaster also prompted improvements in crew training and emergency preparedness, ensuring that crews were better equipped to handle similar situations in the future.

One of the most enduring aspects of the MS Estonia tragedy is the impact it had on the survivors and the families of the victims. The trauma experienced by those who survived the sinking and the grief of those who lost loved ones have left lasting scars. Efforts to commemorate the victims and support the survivors have been ongoing. Memorials have been established in Estonia, Sweden, and Finland, and annual commemorative events are held to honor the memory of those who perished.

The wreck of the MS Estonia lies at a depth of about 80 meters (260 feet) in the Baltic Sea. Due to the sensitivity of the site and the tragic nature of the disaster, the governments of Estonia, Finland, and Sweden have declared it a protected maritime grave, restricting access to the wreck. However, the site has been the subject of various exploration efforts, both official and unofficial, aimed at further understanding the circumstances of the sinking and addressing lingering questions.

The MS Estonia disaster remains a sobering reminder of the potential dangers of maritime travel and the importance of robust safety measures. The tragedy has left a profound legacy, influencing maritime policy and safety practices worldwide. It serves as a case study in the need for continual vigilance and improvement in the design, operation, and regulation of passenger ships. The human cost of the disaster, with the loss of 852 lives, underscores the devastating impact of such events on individuals, families, and communities. The memory of the MS Estonia and its passengers endures, serving as a poignant reminder of the fragility of human life and the enduring quest for safety and resilience in the face of adversity.

# Chapter 15: SS Arctic

The SS Arctic was a luxury paddle steamship that met a tragic end in 1854, marking one of the most devastating maritime disasters of the 19th century. The loss of the SS Arctic not only resulted in significant loss of life but also had profound implications for maritime safety regulations and public perception of transatlantic travel. The disaster occurred on September 27, 1854, when the SS Arctic collided with the French steamship SS Vesta in dense fog off the coast of Newfoundland. The ensuing chaos, inadequate lifeboat capacity, and failures in emergency procedures led to the deaths of 322 of the 408 people on board.

Launched in 1850, the SS Arctic was part of the Collins Line, an American shipping company founded by Edward Knight Collins. The Collins Line was established to compete with the British Cunard Line for dominance in the lucrative transatlantic passenger trade. The Arctic was one of four paddle steamers built for the Collins Line, all of which were known for their speed, luxury, and innovative design. The Arctic, specifically, was 284 feet long and 45 feet wide, with a displacement of 2,856 tons. She was powered by side paddle wheels and could reach speeds of up to 13 knots, making her one of the fastest ships of her time. The ship was designed to carry 200 first-class passengers, 150 second-class passengers, and 200 steerage passengers, along with a crew of 135.

The Arctic set sail on her maiden voyage on October 26, 1850, from New York to Liverpool. She quickly gained a reputation for speed and comfort, offering amenities that were considered luxurious for the time, including spacious cabins, elegant dining facilities, and plush lounges. The success of the Collins Line ships, including the Arctic, was a source of national pride for the United States, as they demonstrated American technological prowess and could compete with the best that Europe had to offer. However, the Collins Line ships were not without their problems. The Arctic and her sister ships were known for their high operating costs and maintenance issues. Their powerful engines and high speeds put significant strain on their structures, leading to frequent repairs and mechanical failures. Despite these issues, the Arctic continued to be a popular choice for transatlantic travel due to her reputation for speed and luxury.

On September 20, 1854, the SS Arctic departed Liverpool for New York on what was supposed to be another routine voyage. The ship was under the command of Captain James Luce, a veteran mariner with extensive experience in transatlantic navigation. Among the passengers were some prominent figures, including Edward Collins' wife and two of their children. The weather conditions were generally favorable at the start of the voyage, but as the Arctic approached the Grand Banks off Newfoundland, the weather deteriorated, and a dense fog set in. Navigating in such conditions was challenging and required extreme caution. Despite the limited visibility, the Arctic continued to steam at a relatively high speed, a common practice at the time for ships trying to maintain tight schedules and avoid delays.

On the morning of September 27, 1854, the Arctic was making her way through the foggy waters when, at around noon, she collided with the SS Vesta, a much smaller iron-hulled French steamship. The Vesta, which was also navigating through the fog, struck the Arctic on her starboard side, creating a gaping hole below the waterline. The collision was catastrophic for both vessels, but the impact was particularly devastating for the Arctic due to her wooden hull. The immediate aftermath of the collision was chaotic. Water began to flood the Arctic's engine room and lower compartments rapidly. Captain Luce ordered the ship to be turned towards land in an attempt to beach her and save as many lives as possible. However, the damage was too severe, and it quickly became apparent that the ship was sinking.

As the situation on board deteriorated, the lack of adequate lifeboat capacity and poor emergency procedures became glaringly evident. The Arctic, like many ships of her era, was not equipped with enough lifeboats to accommodate all passengers and crew. There were only six lifeboats on board, which could hold about 180 people in total, far short of the number needed for everyone on the ship. Panic ensued as passengers and crew scrambled for the limited lifeboat spaces. In the ensuing chaos, discipline broke down, and many of the lifeboats were launched only partially filled or capsized due to overcrowding. There were reports of crew members abandoning their posts and securing places in the lifeboats at the expense of the passengers, including women and children.

Captain Luce attempted to maintain order and oversee the evacuation, but his efforts were largely in vain. The ship's officers were unable to effectively manage the evacuation, and the situation quickly descended into a free-for-all. Some passengers and crew clung to debris or makeshift rafts in a desperate bid for survival. The Arctic continued to take on water and, after about four hours, she finally sank beneath the waves. Of the 408 people on board, only 86 survived, most of whom were crew members. The majority of the passengers, including all the women and children, perished in the disaster. Captain Luce survived by clinging to a piece of wreckage and was later rescued by a passing ship.

The loss of the SS Arctic was a national tragedy and had a profound impact on public opinion regarding maritime safety. The disaster exposed the deficiencies in ship design, lifeboat provisions, and emergency procedures. The inadequate lifeboat capacity was a particularly glaring issue, highlighting the need for regulatory changes to ensure that ships carried enough lifeboats for all passengers and crew. The public outcry following the disaster led to increased scrutiny of maritime safety practices and regulations. In the United States and Britain, there were calls for reforms to improve the safety of transatlantic travel. These included stricter standards for lifeboat capacity, improved training for crew members in emergency procedures, and better maintenance and inspection of ships.

Despite the significant loss of life, there were no immediate regulatory changes following the Arctic disaster. It would take several more high-profile maritime accidents before meaningful reforms were enacted. However, the sinking of the Arctic did contribute to the growing awareness of the need for better safety measures and the eventual development of more comprehensive maritime safety regulations. The Collins Line, already struggling with high operating costs and competition from the Cunard Line, was severely impacted by the loss of the Arctic. The financial and reputational damage from the disaster was a significant blow to the company. The Collins Line continued to operate for a few more years but was eventually forced into bankruptcy in 1858, marking the end of its brief but notable presence in the transatlantic shipping industry.

The legacy of the SS Arctic disaster is a sobering reminder of the dangers of maritime travel in the 19th century and the human cost of inadequate safety measures. The tragedy underscored the importance of ensuring that ships were properly equipped and maintained and that crews were adequately trained to handle emergencies. It also highlighted the need for regulatory oversight to protect the lives of passengers and crew. In the years following the disaster, the story of the SS Arctic has been recounted in numerous books, articles, and documentaries, serving as a cautionary tale and a call to action for improved maritime safety.

# Chapter 16: SS Mont-Blanc

The SS Mont-Blanc disaster, which occurred on December 6, 1917, is one of the most catastrophic maritime incidents in history, known for causing the largest man-made explosion prior to the development of nuclear weapons. This tragic event, commonly referred to as the Halifax Explosion, took place in the harbor of Halifax, Nova Scotia, Canada. The explosion resulted from the collision of the SS Mont-Blanc, a French cargo ship loaded with high explosives, and the Norwegian vessel SS Imo. The resulting blast killed approximately 2,000 people, injured around 9,000, and caused extensive damage to the city of Halifax.

The SS Mont-Blanc was a 3,121-ton French steamship built in 1899. She was initially designed as a general cargo ship but had been requisitioned by the French government during World War I to transport military supplies. On her fateful voyage, the Mont-Blanc was carrying a highly volatile cargo consisting of benzol, picric acid, TNT, and guncotton. The total weight of the explosives on board was about 2,925 metric tons, making her a floating bomb. The ship was en route from New York to Bordeaux, France, via Halifax, which served as a key staging point for transatlantic convoys during the war.

The other vessel involved in the disaster, the SS Imo, was a Norwegian steamship built in 1889. Originally named Runic, she was later renamed and operated as a transport ship for the Belgian Relief Commission, carrying food and supplies to war-torn Europe. On December 6, 1917, the Imo was in Halifax Harbor to refuel before heading to New York to load relief supplies.

The events leading up to the collision and subsequent explosion began early in the morning. The Mont-Blanc arrived outside Halifax Harbor on the evening of December 5 but was unable to enter the harbor before the anti-submarine nets were raised for the night. Consequently, she anchored outside the harbor and waited for permission to enter the next morning. Meanwhile, the Imo was preparing to leave Halifax Harbor and was navigating through the Narrows, a strait connecting the outer harbor to the Bedford Basin.

On the morning of December 6, the harbor was busy with ship traffic. The Imo, running behind schedule, was traveling at a higher speed than usual. As she entered the Narrows, she encountered the Mont-Blanc, which was making her way towards the Bedford Basin. Due to a series of misunderstandings and miscommunications between the pilots and captains of both vessels, they ended up on a collision course. Despite attempts to avoid each other, the Imo struck the Mont-Blanc on her starboard side at 8:45 AM.

The collision itself did not cause an immediate explosion, but it ruptured several drums of benzol stored on the deck of the Mont-Blanc. The leaking benzol quickly formed a flammable vapor cloud. The crew of the Mont-Blanc, realizing the imminent danger, abandoned ship and rowed to shore, desperately warning people to flee the area. As the Mont-Blanc drifted towards the Halifax waterfront, a fire ignited the benzol vapors, leading to a massive explosion at 9:04 AM.

The explosion was cataclysmic. The blast had an estimated force equivalent to 2.9 kilotons of TNT, creating a shockwave that radiated outward from the epicenter. The immediate impact obliterated the Mont-Blanc, vaporizing her and sending fragments of the ship flying in all directions. The explosion produced a powerful shockwave that shattered windows, collapsed buildings, and caused widespread destruction within a 2.5-mile radius. A towering column of smoke and debris rose nearly 20,000 feet into the air.

The human toll was immense. Approximately 2,000 people were killed instantly or succumbed to their injuries shortly after the explosion. The blast left about 9,000 others wounded, many with severe burns, lacerations, and broken bones. The explosion's force was so great that it caused injuries up to 100 kilometers away. Among the dead were many children, as schools and homes were destroyed. The blast also killed members of the crews of both ships, harbor workers, and civilians who had gathered to watch the burning ship.

The devastation in Halifax was unprecedented. Entire neighborhoods were leveled, and more than 1,600 homes were destroyed, leaving thousands homeless. The blast also caused fires to break out throughout the city, further exacerbating the destruction and hampering rescue efforts. The Halifax Explosion was compounded by the fact that it occurred during the winter, subjecting survivors and rescuers to harsh weather conditions. A blizzard struck the region the following day, complicating the rescue and recovery operations and adding to the misery of the survivors.

The response to the disaster was swift and coordinated, involving both local and international aid. The Canadian military, along with local police, firefighters, and medical personnel, immediately began rescue operations. Temporary hospitals and shelters were established to care for the injured and displaced. The city of Boston, in particular, played a significant role in the relief efforts, sending medical teams, supplies, and financial aid. The bonds formed between Halifax and Boston during this crisis endure to this day, symbolized by the annual gift of a Christmas tree from Nova Scotia to Boston as a token of gratitude.

Investigations into the disaster were launched to determine the causes and assign responsibility. A commission of inquiry was established, and it concluded that both the Mont-Blanc and the Imo had contributed to the collision through navigational errors and miscommunications. The inquiry also highlighted the lack of proper procedures for handling hazardous cargo in a busy harbor. While no criminal charges were brought against the crews or the shipping companies, the disaster underscored the need for stricter regulations and better safety practices in maritime transport.

The Halifax Explosion had far-reaching consequences beyond the immediate loss of life and property. It prompted changes in harbor regulations and ship handling procedures, particularly concerning the transport of dangerous goods. The disaster also led to advancements in emergency response and medical care, as the scale of the tragedy necessitated innovations in trauma treatment and disaster management.

Memorials and commemorations for the victims of the Halifax Explosion have been established over the years, ensuring that the memory of those who perished is preserved. The Fort Needham Memorial Bell Tower, located in a park overlooking the explosion site, serves as a poignant reminder of the tragedy. Every year on December 6, ceremonies are held to honor the memory of the victims and to reflect on the resilience of the Halifax community.

The Halifax Explosion remains a significant event in Canadian history, both for its devastating impact and for the lessons learned from the tragedy. The disaster highlighted the dangers of transporting hazardous materials and underscored the importance of communication and safety in maritime operations. It also showcased the strength and solidarity of a community in the face of overwhelming adversity. The story of the SS Mont-Blanc and the Halifax Explosion is a testament to the destructive power of human error and the enduring spirit of recovery and remembrance.

# Chapter 17: Bermuda Triangle

The Bermuda Triangle, often referred to as the Devil's Triangle, is a loosely defined region in the western part of the North Atlantic Ocean, covering an area of approximately 500,000 to 1,500,000 square miles. The triangle is bounded by points in Miami, Florida; Bermuda; and Puerto Rico, forming a roughly triangular shape. This area has gained notoriety over the decades due to an unusually high number of aircraft and ships that have mysteriously disappeared while traversing it. The intrigue surrounding the Bermuda Triangle began in the mid-20th century, with numerous theories ranging from the scientifically plausible to the wildly speculative attempting to explain the mysterious disappearances.

The legend of the Bermuda Triangle can be traced back to an article published in the Miami Herald on September 17, 1950, by Edward Van Winkle Jones. Two years later, Fate magazine published an article by George X. Sand covering the loss of several planes and ships, including the mysterious disappearance of Flight 19, a squadron of five U.S. Navy TBM Avenger torpedo bombers, on December 5, 1945. Flight 19 departed from Fort Lauderdale, Florida, on a routine training mission. Under the command of Lieutenant Charles C. Taylor, the flight encountered navigational difficulties, reported by Taylor in a series of confused radio transmissions. Despite rescue efforts, neither the planes nor the 14 airmen were ever found. This incident significantly contributed to the Bermuda Triangle mythos.

Another significant event that fueled the Bermuda Triangle mystery was the disappearance of the SS Marine Sulphur Queen in February 1963. The SS Marine Sulphur Queen was a T2 tanker loaded with molten sulfur. She was last heard from on February 4, 1963, when she sent a routine radio message while en route from Beaumont, Texas, to Norfolk, Virginia. The ship and her 39 crew members vanished without a trace. Despite an extensive search by the Coast Guard, no wreckage was ever found, adding to the growing list of unexplained incidents within the Bermuda Triangle.

The legend was further popularized by Charles Berlitz in his 1974 bestseller "The Bermuda Triangle." Berlitz, known for his works on paranormal phenomena, suggested that the disappearances were connected to supernatural or extraterrestrial activities. Berlitz's book sparked widespread interest and led to a proliferation of theories attempting to explain the mysterious occurrences in the region. These theories have ranged from plausible scientific explanations to more fantastical ideas.

Among the more scientific theories is the suggestion that the Bermuda Triangle is subject to unusual environmental conditions. One such theory posits that the area is prone to rogue waves, which are extremely large and sudden ocean waves capable of sinking ships and overwhelming aircraft. Rogue waves can reach heights of up to 100 feet and have been documented in various parts of the world's oceans. Their sudden appearance and immense power could easily account for the loss of vessels within the Bermuda Triangle.

Another environmental factor often cited is the region's susceptibility to powerful and unpredictable weather patterns, including hurricanes and tropical storms. The Bermuda Triangle is located in an area where such weather events are common, and these storms can produce sudden, violent changes in weather conditions. Historically, many of the disappearances attributed to the Bermuda Triangle have occurred during periods of bad weather, suggesting that natural meteorological phenomena play a significant role.

The presence of large quantities of methane hydrates on the ocean floor is another scientific explanation that has been proposed. Methane hydrates are crystalline structures that contain large amounts of methane gas. When these hydrates decompose, they can release vast quantities of gas, potentially reducing the density of the water and causing ships to sink. Additionally, the release of methane gas into the atmosphere could affect the buoyancy and flight capabilities of aircraft. This phenomenon, known as the "methane gas hypothesis," could explain some of the sudden and unexplained losses within the Bermuda Triangle.

Magnetic anomalies have also been suggested as a possible explanation for the Bermuda Triangle mysteries. The area is known for having variations in magnetic declination, which is the angle between magnetic north and true north. These anomalies could potentially interfere with navigational instruments, leading to confusion and disorientation among pilots and ship captains. This could result in navigational errors that might cause vessels to become lost or crash.

Despite the numerous scientific explanations, the Bermuda Triangle has also been the subject of many more speculative and sensational theories. One of the most famous is the suggestion that the area is a portal to another dimension or a time warp, capable of transporting objects and people into another realm or time period. This theory, while lacking empirical evidence, has captured the imagination of many and continues to be a popular explanation for the mysterious disappearances.

Another widely discussed but scientifically unsupported theory is that the Bermuda Triangle is the site of an underwater extraterrestrial base. Proponents of this idea argue that advanced alien technology could be responsible for the sudden and unexplained disappearances. This theory gained traction in the 1970s and 1980s, fueled by reports of UFO sightings in the region and the popularity of science fiction literature and media.

Some theories even hark back to the lost city of Atlantis. Proponents of this idea suggest that the Bermuda Triangle is the location of the sunken city and that remnants of Atlantean technology, such as powerful energy crystals, could be responsible for the disruptions causing ships and planes to vanish. This idea, while appealing to those with a penchant for ancient mysteries, remains purely speculative and without any archaeological or geological evidence.

In reality, the number of incidents reported in the Bermuda Triangle is not significantly higher than in any other heavily traveled region of the world. The U.S. Coast Guard and other authorities have repeatedly stated that the vast majority of incidents can be attributed to human error, mechanical failure, and natural environmental factors. The waters of the Bermuda Triangle are part of a heavily traveled shipping route, and the high volume of traffic increases the likelihood of accidents. Furthermore, the tropical climate of the region contributes to severe weather conditions, which can pose risks to ships and aircraft.

Statistical analysis has shown that the rate of incidents in the Bermuda Triangle is comparable to that of other parts of the world. Many of the disappearances that have been sensationalized are, upon closer investigation, explainable by mundane causes. For example, the loss of Flight 19 can be attributed to navigational errors compounded by bad weather and limited fuel. The disappearance of the SS Marine Sulphur Queen is believed to have been caused by structural issues and poor maintenance, leading to her sinking.

Despite the lack of empirical evidence supporting the more fantastical theories, the Bermuda Triangle remains a cultural phenomenon and a source of enduring fascination. It has been featured in countless books, documentaries, and movies, each contributing to the mythos and mystery of the region. The allure of the unknown and the human tendency to seek explanations for unexplained events have ensured that the legend of the Bermuda Triangle continues to captivate the public imagination.

In recent years, advancements in technology and underwater exploration have allowed scientists to investigate the region more thoroughly. Sonar mapping, deep-sea submersibles, and improved satellite tracking have provided valuable data that helps to demystify the area. These tools have revealed the complexities of the ocean floor, including underwater currents, geological formations, and other factors that can contribute to navigational challenges.

While the Bermuda Triangle remains a subject of intrigue, it is important to approach the topic with a critical and scientific mindset. The combination of natural environmental factors, human error, and the high volume of traffic in the area provides a plausible explanation for the incidents that have occurred. The enduring mystery of the Bermuda Triangle serves as a reminder of the power of nature and the limits of human technology and understanding.

# Chapter 18: RMS Lusitania

The RMS Lusitania, a British ocean liner owned by the Cunard Line, was one of the most famous ships of the early 20th century. Launched in 1906, the Lusitania was celebrated for its speed, luxury, and technological advancements. It represented a pinnacle of maritime engineering and comfort, intended to compete with rival German vessels in the lucrative transatlantic passenger trade. At 787 feet long and weighing over 31,000 tons, the Lusitania was one of the largest and fastest ships in the world, capable of crossing the Atlantic in under five days.

The Lusitania's story, however, is marked by a tragic and controversial end during World War I. On May 7, 1915, the ship was torpedoed by the German U-boat U-20 off the coast of Ireland, leading to the deaths of 1,198 of the 1,959 people on board. The sinking of the Lusitania had profound implications, both immediate and long-lasting, influencing public opinion and international policy during the war.

At the time of its launch, the Lusitania was designed to be the epitome of luxury and speed. Its construction featured innovative technologies, including a quadruple-screw turbine engine, which allowed it to achieve speeds exceeding 25 knots. This speed was not only a matter of pride but also a strategic advantage in the highly competitive transatlantic passenger market. The Lusitania, along with its sister ship, the Mauretania, was intended to showcase British maritime prowess and attract wealthy passengers who demanded the highest standards of comfort and service.

The Lusitania's interiors were lavishly appointed, featuring elegant dining rooms, spacious staterooms, and public areas decorated with fine woodwork, tapestries, and artworks. Passengers could enjoy amenities such as a library, a reading and writing room, and an array of dining options that catered to the tastes of the era's elite. The ship also boasted state-of-the-art safety features, including watertight compartments and advanced navigation systems, which contributed to its reputation as a marvel of modern engineering.

Despite its reputation, the Lusitania was not immune to the dangers of war. When World War I broke out in 1914, the seas became a perilous place for commercial vessels. Germany had declared the waters around the British Isles a war zone, warning that Allied ships would be targeted by their submarines. The British Admiralty, in turn, advised passenger ships to avoid the area or to take precautions such as zigzagging to evade detection.

On its final voyage, the Lusitania departed New York for Liverpool on May 1, 1915. Despite warnings from the German embassy published in American newspapers, many passengers and crew believed that the Lusitania, given its speed and the British naval presence, could avoid any threat from German submarines. The ship carried 1,959 people, including 1,266 passengers and 693 crew members, as well as a significant cargo that controversially included munitions and other war materials.

The crossing proceeded uneventfully until the Lusitania reached the waters off the southern coast of Ireland. On the afternoon of May 7, the ship was nearing its destination, traveling along a course that brought it within range of German U-boat patrols. Captain William Thomas Turner had received warnings about submarine activity in the area but maintained a straight course, believing the ship's speed would protect it.

At approximately 2:10 PM, U-20, commanded by Captain Walther Schwieger, spotted the Lusitania and fired a single torpedo. The torpedo struck the starboard side of the ship near the bow, causing a massive explosion. Almost immediately, a second, more powerful explosion occurred, likely caused by the ignition of the ship's munitions cargo. The combined blasts created a catastrophic breach in the hull, and the Lusitania began to list sharply to starboard and sink by the bow.

Panic and chaos ensued as passengers and crew rushed to the lifeboats. The severe list of the ship made it difficult to launch many of the lifeboats, and only six of the 48 were successfully deployed. Within 18 minutes, the Lusitania had sunk beneath the waves, leaving hundreds of people struggling in the cold Atlantic waters. Nearby ships, including the trawler Bluebell and the armed merchant cruiser Juno, responded to the distress calls and rescued many survivors, but the loss of life was immense.

The sinking of the Lusitania sent shockwaves around the world. In Britain, it was seen as a heinous act of aggression by Germany, fueling anti-German sentiment and bolstering support for the war effort. In the United States, the event provoked widespread outrage, though the country remained officially neutral at that time. President Woodrow Wilson's administration issued strong protests to the German government, demanding an end to unrestricted submarine warfare.

The incident also sparked controversy and debate. Some argued that the Lusitania was a legitimate target due to its cargo of munitions, while others contended that the attack on a civilian passenger liner was a war crime. The British government conducted an inquiry, led by Lord Mersey, which concluded that the primary responsibility for the disaster lay with the German U-boat commander. However, the inquiry also criticized the Admiralty for not providing sufficient protection to the Lusitania and questioned the wisdom of allowing the ship to carry such a dangerous cargo.

The sinking of the Lusitania had a lasting impact on public opinion and wartime policy. It contributed to the growing perception of Germany as a ruthless enemy willing to violate international law and norms of warfare. This perception played a role in the eventual entry of the United States into the war in 1917, following renewed German submarine attacks on American ships. The event also highlighted the vulnerabilities of civilian vessels in wartime and led to changes in naval strategy and ship design to enhance safety and survivability.

In the years following the disaster, the Lusitania became a symbol of the tragic consequences of war. Memorials were erected to honor the victims, and numerous books, articles, and films recounted the story of the ship and its fateful final voyage. The wreck of the Lusitania remains on the seabed off the coast of Ireland, a poignant reminder of the human cost of conflict and the enduring mysteries of maritime history.

To this day, researchers and historians continue to study the Lusitania, seeking to uncover new details about the circumstances of its sinking and the broader implications for naval warfare and international relations during World War I. The ship's story is a testament to the complexities and dangers of the sea, as well as the enduring fascination with the dramatic and often tragic events that unfold upon it.

# Chapter 19: HMS Bounty

The HMS Bounty, a replica of the original 18th-century British Royal Navy ship, gained fame both for its historical significance and its prominent role in Hollywood films, notably the 1962 movie "Mutiny on the Bounty" and the 1984 film starring Mel Gibson. The original Bounty was launched in 1784, and its voyage to Tahiti in 1787 to transport breadfruit plants to the Caribbean became legendary due to the infamous mutiny led by Fletcher Christian against Captain William Bligh. The replica Bounty, built in 1960 for the 1962 film, became a beloved educational and sailing vessel, often touring ports around the world and participating in maritime events.

In 2012, the replica HMS Bounty faced a tragic end when it encountered Hurricane Sandy, one of the most devastating and expansive hurricanes in recent history. The disaster that befell the Bounty during this hurricane was a maritime catastrophe that highlighted the perils faced by even experienced sailors and well-equipped ships in the face of natural forces. The sinking of the Bounty and the subsequent loss of life marked a somber chapter in the ship's storied history, raising questions about decision-making, preparedness, and safety at sea.

The journey that led to the Bounty's demise began on October 25, 2012, when the ship departed from New London, Connecticut, bound for St. Petersburg, Florida. Captain Robin Walbridge, an experienced mariner with a deep understanding of the Bounty, was at the helm. Despite forecasts of the approaching Hurricane Sandy, Captain Walbridge believed that the ship could navigate safely around the storm. His plan was to sail southeast to avoid the hurricane's projected path and then head west once clear of the storm.

The Bounty was a robust ship, equipped with modern navigational aids and safety equipment, but it was also a wooden vessel, inherently more vulnerable to the extreme conditions of a hurricane. The decision to set sail despite the storm warnings was later scrutinized, as it ultimately placed the ship and its crew in grave danger. Captain Walbridge's confidence in the Bounty's seaworthiness and his strategy to outmaneuver the storm reflected his deep attachment to the vessel and his belief in its capabilities.

As Hurricane Sandy advanced, it grew in strength and size, becoming a massive system with hurricane-force winds extending hundreds of miles from its center. The Bounty's path took it into increasingly perilous waters, where the seas grew rougher and the winds more intense. By October 28, the ship was battling high waves and strong winds as it attempted to navigate around the storm. The crew, consisting of 16 members, worked tirelessly to manage the ship and maintain its course, but the worsening conditions posed severe challenges.

On the evening of October 28, the situation aboard the Bounty deteriorated rapidly. The ship began taking on water, and the crew struggled to keep the pumps running and the bilge clear. Despite their efforts, the flooding became uncontrollable. The combination of the powerful storm surge, high waves, and the ship's wooden construction proved overwhelming. By the early hours of October 29, it became clear that the Bounty was in imminent danger of sinking.

Captain Walbridge made the decision to abandon ship, ordering the crew to don survival suits and prepare to evacuate. The crew faced the daunting task of launching lifeboats and entering the turbulent waters of the Atlantic Ocean amidst the raging storm. As they attempted to abandon the Bounty, the ship continued to list and sink, making the evacuation even more hazardous. The crew members, many of whom had bonded over their shared experiences aboard the Bounty, faced a terrifying ordeal as they fought for their lives in the storm-tossed sea.

The U.S. Coast Guard received a distress signal from the Bounty and immediately launched a rescue operation. Helicopters and rescue vessels were dispatched to the scene, but the extreme weather conditions and remote location made the mission exceptionally challenging. Rescuers battled high winds, heavy rain, and rough seas as they searched for the crew members. Despite these difficulties, the Coast Guard managed to locate and rescue 14 of the 16 crew members.

Tragically, two lives were lost in the disaster. Claudene Christian, a descendant of Fletcher Christian, the leader of the original Bounty mutiny, was found unresponsive in the water and later pronounced dead. Captain Robin Walbridge was never found, despite extensive search efforts. His loss was deeply felt by the maritime community and those who knew him as a skilled and passionate sailor dedicated to the Bounty and its legacy.

The sinking of the HMS Bounty prompted widespread reflection and analysis within the maritime world. The incident raised critical questions about decision-making in the face of severe weather, the responsibilities of ship captains, and the adequacy of safety measures on traditional and replica vessels. Investigations by the National Transportation Safety Board (NTSB) and the Coast Guard examined the circumstances leading up to the disaster, including Captain Walbridge's decision to sail into the path of Hurricane Sandy.

The NTSB report, released in 2014, concluded that the decision to sail into the hurricane was the primary cause of the sinking. It highlighted the risks associated with such a decision and emphasized the importance of adhering to safety protocols and avoiding unnecessary exposure to severe weather. The report also called for improved safety measures and oversight for vessels like the Bounty, which operate in both historical and educational contexts.

In the wake of the disaster, there was an outpouring of support and condolences from the maritime community, historians, and the general public. The loss of the Bounty was mourned not only as the end of a beloved ship but also as a reminder of the unpredictable and often unforgiving nature of the sea. Memorials and tributes honored the memory of the lost crew members and celebrated the ship's contributions to maritime history and education.

The legacy of the HMS Bounty endures through the memories of those who sailed on her, the films and media that featured her, and the ongoing discussions about maritime safety and heritage preservation. The story of the Bounty serves as a poignant reminder of the delicate balance between human ambition, the allure of the sea, and the formidable power of nature. It underscores the need for respect, caution, and preparedness in the face of the ocean's vast and often unpredictable expanse.

# Chapter 20: SS Morro Castle

The SS Morro Castle was a luxury passenger liner operated by the Ward Line, officially known as the New York and Cuba Mail Steamship Company. Launched in 1930, the ship was named after the fortress guarding the entrance to Havana Bay in Cuba. It was designed to provide a glamorous and comfortable voyage between New York City and Havana, catering to affluent passengers seeking leisure and luxury. The ship's construction featured modern amenities for its time, including elegant dining rooms, spacious staterooms, and an array of recreational facilities.

On September 5, 1934, the Morro Castle embarked on what was supposed to be a routine voyage from Havana to New York. The journey proceeded smoothly until the night of September 7, when tragedy struck. At approximately 2:50 AM on September 8, as the ship sailed off the coast of New Jersey, a fire broke out in a storage locker. Within minutes, the fire rapidly spread through the ship's superstructure, fueled by highly flammable materials and exacerbated by strong winds.

The situation aboard the Morro Castle quickly became chaotic and desperate. Many passengers were asleep when the fire began, and the crew's initial attempts to combat the blaze were hampered by poor training, inadequate equipment, and a lack of effective leadership. The ship's fire suppression systems failed to function properly, and the flames engulfed the wooden interiors and flammable furnishings with alarming speed. Panic ensued as passengers and crew members struggled to find a means of escape.

One of the critical failures during the disaster was the lack of clear communication and emergency procedures. The ship's radio operator managed to send a distress signal, but the message lacked crucial details about the ship's exact location and the severity of the situation. As the fire intensified, thick smoke filled the corridors and cabins, making it difficult for passengers to navigate their way to the lifeboats. The crew's attempts to launch the lifeboats were hampered by the ship's listing and the intense heat, resulting in many lifeboats being either inaccessible or unusable.

Survivors later recounted harrowing tales of their efforts to escape the inferno. Some passengers and crew members jumped into the cold Atlantic waters, clinging to debris or makeshift flotation devices as they awaited rescue. The intense heat and smoke rendered large sections of the ship uninhabitable, and those who remained on board faced a grim struggle for survival. The ship's structure itself began to buckle under the relentless assault of the flames, further complicating rescue efforts.

Rescue operations were mounted swiftly in response to the Morro Castle's distress signal. Coast Guard vessels, commercial ships, and fishing boats converged on the scene, working tirelessly to save as many lives as possible. Despite these efforts, the fire claimed the lives of 137 passengers and crew members. The survivors, many of whom had suffered severe burns and smoke inhalation, were brought to shore and received medical treatment. The ordeal left an indelible mark on all those who experienced it, as well as on the broader maritime community.

The SS Morro Castle disaster prompted a comprehensive investigation into the causes and contributing factors of the fire. The inquiry revealed a series of deficiencies in the ship's design, construction, and operation. Among the key findings were the inadequate fire suppression systems, the use of highly flammable materials in the ship's interiors, and the lack of effective fire drills and emergency procedures for the crew. The investigation also highlighted the need for better training and preparedness for maritime emergencies.

One of the most controversial aspects of the Morro Castle disaster was the role of the ship's captain and senior officers. Captain Robert Willmott, who had been in command of the Morro Castle, died under mysterious circumstances just hours before the fire broke out. His sudden death left the ship under the command of Chief Officer William Warms, whose leadership during the crisis was widely criticized. The exact cause of Captain Willmott's death was never conclusively determined, but it added a layer of intrigue and suspicion to the already tragic events.

The aftermath of the Morro Castle disaster led to significant changes in maritime safety regulations and practices. The incident served as a catalyst for the implementation of stricter fire safety standards for passenger ships, including the use of fire-resistant materials in ship construction, improved fire detection and suppression systems, and mandatory fire drills and training for crew members. The lessons learned from the Morro Castle tragedy were instrumental in shaping modern maritime safety protocols and ensuring that similar disasters would be less likely to occur in the future.

The burned-out hulk of the Morro Castle eventually ran aground on the New Jersey shore near Asbury Park, where it remained for several months before being dismantled and scrapped. The sight of the charred wreckage became a grim tourist attraction, drawing crowds who came to witness the aftermath of the disaster. The images of the burned-out ship and the stories of those who survived the inferno left a lasting impression on the public consciousness, reinforcing the need for greater vigilance and safety in maritime travel.

In the years following the disaster, the SS Morro Castle continued to capture the public's imagination, inspiring books, documentaries, and academic studies. The story of the ship and its tragic end serves as a stark reminder of the potential dangers of sea travel and the importance of rigorous safety standards. The legacy of the Morro Castle lives on in the ongoing efforts to improve maritime safety and protect the lives of those who travel by sea.

The SS Morro Castle disaster remains one of the most significant maritime tragedies of the 20th century. It underscores the vulnerability of ships and their passengers to the destructive power of fire, the critical importance of effective emergency response measures, and the enduring need for vigilance and preparedness in the face of potential disasters. The lessons learned from the Morro Castle have helped to shape the safety protocols that govern modern maritime travel, ensuring that the mistakes of the past are not repeated. The memory of the lives lost in the inferno serves as a poignant reminder of the human cost of such tragedies and the ongoing commitment to safeguarding those who venture out to sea.

# Chapter 21: SS Andrea Gail

The story of the SS Andrea Gail is one of the most tragic and haunting maritime disasters in recent history. The Andrea Gail was a commercial fishing vessel based out of Gloucester, Massachusetts, a town known for its long-standing fishing industry and the hardy, skilled fishermen who call it home. Built in 1978, the 72-foot longliner was specifically designed for swordfishing, a perilous occupation that often takes crews far out into the open ocean in search of their catch. The vessel and its crew became famous not just for the calamity that befell them, but also because of the book "The Perfect Storm" by Sebastian Junger, and the subsequent film adaptation.

In late September 1991, the Andrea Gail set out from Gloucester for the Grand Banks of Newfoundland, one of the world's richest fishing grounds. Captain Frank W. "Billy" Tyne Jr. was at the helm, a seasoned fisherman with extensive experience navigating the treacherous waters of the North Atlantic. His crew consisted of five men: Robert "Bobby" Shatford, David "Sully" Sullivan, Michael "Bugsy" Moran, Dale "Murph" Murphy, and Alfred Pierre. All were eager to return with a lucrative haul of swordfish, which had become increasingly scarce closer to shore.

The fishing trip started like many others, with the crew setting their lines and enduring the tough conditions of the open sea. However, as the days passed, the weather began to deteriorate. Unbeknownst to the crew of the Andrea Gail, a unique and extremely dangerous weather pattern was forming. Meteorologists would later refer to this as "The Perfect Storm," a confluence of three separate weather systems: a low-pressure system from the Great Lakes, a high-pressure system from Canada, and Hurricane Grace, which was moving up the eastern seaboard. The collision of these systems created an extraordinarily powerful and unpredictable storm.

On October 26, 1991, Captain Tyne made the decision to head back to Gloucester. With their ice machine broken and concerns about preserving their catch, the crew faced the dilemma of risking the storm to save their haul. The decision to return through what was shaping up to be one of the most intense storms ever recorded was fraught with danger, but the alternative seemed equally dire. As they made their way back, the storm rapidly intensified, producing waves reported to be over 100 feet high and winds exceeding 70 miles per hour.

The Andrea Gail's final radio contact was a brief, chilling message: "She's comin' on, boys, and she's comin' on strong." This communication, made on October 28, 1991, to another fishing vessel, the Hannah Boden, was the last anyone heard from the Andrea Gail. Despite efforts to reach them, all subsequent attempts at communication failed. The storm's ferocity made rescue operations nearly impossible. The vessel and its crew were officially declared missing on November 6, 1991, after an extensive but ultimately fruitless search by the Coast Guard and other vessels.

In the aftermath of the storm, debris from the Andrea Gail was found, including a fuel tank, an emergency position-indicating radio beacon (EPIRB), and other flotsam. These remnants were discovered floating in the ocean, stark evidence of the ship's likely destruction. The exact fate of the vessel remains a mystery, as no bodies or substantial wreckage were ever recovered. The storm's intensity and the vastness of the ocean make it improbable that the full story of what happened to the Andrea Gail will ever be known.

The impact of the Andrea Gail disaster resonated deeply within the fishing community of Gloucester and beyond. The loss of six men who had gone to sea to make a living was a harsh reminder of the dangers inherent in commercial fishing, an industry that has always balanced on the knife-edge between survival and catastrophe. The families of the crew members were left with grief and unanswered questions, as the sea had taken their loved ones with no trace.

Sebastian Junger's book "The Perfect Storm" brought the story of the Andrea Gail to a wider audience, blending meticulous research with narrative storytelling to capture the harrowing ordeal. The book delves into the lives of the crew members, the nature of the storm, and the broader context of the fishing industry. It became a bestseller and was later adapted into a successful Hollywood film in 2000, starring George Clooney as Captain Billy Tyne. Both the book and the film paid tribute to the bravery of the crew and highlighted the often overlooked perils faced by commercial fishermen.

The story of the Andrea Gail is more than just a tale of a ship lost at sea; it is a powerful narrative about human determination, the unpredictable force of nature, and the relentless pursuit of livelihood. The tragedy underscored the inherent risks of the fishing profession, where individuals confront not just the physical challenges of the job, but also the uncontrollable elements that can turn a routine trip into a life-and-death struggle.

In the years since the disaster, the legacy of the Andrea Gail has continued to influence discussions on maritime safety and the working conditions of commercial fishermen. The incident prompted a closer look at the technology and practices used in the industry, emphasizing the need for better forecasting, communication, and emergency response measures. Modern fishing vessels are now equipped with more advanced navigation and safety equipment, designed to provide better protection against the types of severe weather events that doomed the Andrea Gail.

The story of the SS Andrea Gail remains a poignant reminder of the ocean's unforgiving power. It serves as a memorial to the crew members who perished and a testament to the enduring spirit of those who venture into the depths in search of their catch. Their story is emblematic of the countless fishermen who have faced similar dangers throughout history, risking their lives to bring food to the table and support their communities.

The fishing town of Gloucester continues to honor the memory of the Andrea Gail and its crew. Annual ceremonies and memorials pay tribute to those lost at sea, fostering a sense of solidarity and remembrance among the fishing community. The tale of the Andrea Gail, encapsulated in both literature and film, ensures that the legacy of these men and their fateful voyage endures, reminding future generations of the courage required to face the sea's perils and the unpredictability of nature's wrath.

# Chapter 22: Whale ship Essex

The whale ship Essex's story is one of the most extraordinary and harrowing tales of survival at sea. Launched in 1799 from Nantucket, Massachusetts, the Essex was a 238-ton whaling vessel. The ship, commanded by Captain George Pollard Jr., embarked on what would become its final and most infamous voyage on August 12, 1819. This journey was intended to hunt sperm whales, whose valuable oil was used for lighting and lubrication in an era before petroleum products. Little did the crew know that this expedition would lead to one of the most remarkable maritime disasters and a struggle for survival that would captivate imaginations for centuries to come.

The Essex was typical of the whaling ships of its time, sturdy and well-equipped for long voyages that often lasted two to three years. These ships would travel the vast expanses of the world's oceans in search of sperm whales, primarily in the South Pacific, where these creatures were abundant. The crew of the Essex included 21 men, many of them young and from Nantucket, a town with a deep whaling heritage.

The voyage started uneventfully, with the ship sailing around Cape Horn into the Pacific Ocean. By the autumn of 1820, the Essex had traveled thousands of miles from home and was operating in the remote whaling grounds of the South Pacific, far from any immediate help or rescue. The crew had already faced several challenges, including damage to the ship from a storm, but they were about to encounter an ordeal far more severe.

On November 20, 1820, the Essex was about 2,000 nautical miles west of the Galápagos Islands when the lookout spotted a pod of sperm whales. The crew launched three small whaleboats to pursue and harpoon the whales. While engaged in this hunt, one of the whaleboats was destroyed by a whale's tail. However, the most astonishing event occurred when an unusually large sperm whale, estimated to be 85 feet long, surfaced near the Essex. This whale behaved aggressively, ramming the ship twice with tremendous force.

The first strike by the whale caused significant damage, but the second strike was catastrophic. The massive impact stove in the ship's bow, causing it to take on water rapidly. The Essex began to sink, and the crew scrambled to salvage what they could, including food, water, and navigational instruments, before abandoning ship in the remaining two whaleboats. Their situation was dire, stranded in the middle of the Pacific Ocean with limited supplies and thousands of miles from the nearest land.

For weeks, the crew faced unimaginable hardships. They navigated using rudimentary charts and compasses, aiming for the relatively close Marquesas Islands, but fearing cannibalistic tribes reportedly inhabiting them, they decided to aim for South America instead, a much longer and more arduous journey. The decision was a fateful one, as it meant many more weeks at sea in open boats, exposed to the elements, with dwindling supplies.

The crew's plight worsened as they exhausted their provisions. Dehydration, starvation, and exposure began to take their toll. Desperation set in, and the men were forced to ration their food and water strictly. They supplemented their meager supplies by capturing rainwater and eating whatever fish or birds they could catch. Despite their efforts, conditions deteriorated, and the first of the crew members began to die from the harsh conditions.

As weeks turned into months, the situation grew even more desperate. The surviving crew members were eventually driven to cannibalism, consuming the bodies of their deceased shipmates to stay alive. This grim and horrifying practice was a stark reflection of the extreme circumstances they faced. Drawing lots to determine who would be sacrificed was one of the most harrowing decisions they had to make, highlighting the severe moral and ethical dilemmas that arose in their struggle for survival.

On February 18, 1821, after more than 90 days adrift, the whaleboat containing Captain Pollard and three other survivors was rescued by the whaling ship Dauphin. The crew of the Dauphin was horrified by the sight of the emaciated survivors, who had resorted to cannibalism to stay alive. Another whaleboat, containing First Mate Owen Chase and two others, was rescued a week later by the British ship Indian. The third whaleboat, which had become separated, was never found, and its crew was presumed lost at sea.

In total, only eight of the 21 crew members survived the ordeal. Their rescue marked the end of a grueling and tragic chapter in maritime history. The survivors were eventually taken back to Nantucket, where their return was met with a mix of relief and shock. The details of their ordeal and the extreme measures they took to survive were initially met with disbelief and horror.

Owen Chase, one of the survivors, wrote a detailed account of the ordeal, titled "Narrative of the Most Extraordinary and Distressing Shipwreck of the Whale-Ship Essex." Published in 1821, this account provided a harrowing and vivid depiction of the events, capturing the public's imagination and becoming a significant influence on maritime literature. Chase's narrative was one of the primary sources for Herman Melville's famous novel "Moby-Dick," which explored themes of obsession, the power of nature, and the human struggle for survival.

The story of the Essex and its crew is a profound example of human endurance and the will to survive against insurmountable odds. It also serves as a cautionary tale about the perils of whaling, a dangerous and often deadly occupation. The disaster highlighted the vulnerability of even the most experienced sailors when confronted with the formidable forces of nature and the vast, unforgiving expanse of the open ocean.

The Essex tragedy also had broader implications for the whaling industry. It underscored the need for better safety measures and improved ship design to withstand the hazards of long voyages in treacherous waters. While the industry continued to thrive for several more decades, the lessons learned from the Essex disaster contributed to a growing awareness of the dangers faced by whalers and the importance of preparedness and resilience.

In Nantucket, the memory of the Essex and its ill-fated voyage remains an integral part of the island's rich maritime history. The story is commemorated in museums and through historical markers, serving as a testament to the bravery and resilience of those who ventured into the unknown in pursuit of their livelihood. The tale of the Essex continues to captivate historians, writers, and readers, offering a poignant reminder of the extraordinary challenges and profound mysteries of life at sea.

The legacy of the Essex disaster endures not only through literature and historical accounts but also as a symbol of the relentless and often merciless nature of the ocean. It stands as a powerful narrative of survival, sacrifice, and the human spirit's capacity to endure even the most extreme conditions. The men of the Essex, who faced unimaginable trials and made unthinkable choices, are remembered as both victims of a tragic event and as embodiments of the courage and determination that define the human experience in the face of adversity.

# Chapter 23: HMS Royal George

The HMS Royal George was a first-rate ship of the line in the British Royal Navy, notable for its formidable size and firepower. Launched on September 29, 1756, she was one of the largest warships of her time, boasting 100 guns and serving as a symbol of British naval might. Her construction at Woolwich Dockyard marked a significant achievement in naval architecture, embodying the power and reach of the British Empire during the 18th century. The ship was built during the Seven Years' War, a period of intense maritime conflict that necessitated powerful and heavily armed vessels to protect British interests and engage enemy fleets.

The Royal George saw extensive service throughout her career, participating in numerous naval battles and expeditions. One of her most notable engagements was the Battle of Cape St. Vincent in 1780, where she played a critical role in a decisive victory against the Spanish fleet. Under the command of Admiral Sir George Rodney, the Royal George demonstrated her formidable firepower and the skill of her crew, contributing significantly to the British success. This battle helped to cement her reputation as one of the most powerful and effective ships in the Royal Navy.

However, it is the tragic sinking of the Royal George in 1782 that has etched her name into maritime history. The disaster occurred on August 29, 1782, while the ship was anchored at Spithead, near Portsmouth, for routine maintenance. The ship was being heeled over to allow repairs to be made to her hull below the waterline—a common practice at the time. During this process, the ship's lower deck gun ports were left open, and a combination of factors led to a catastrophic loss of stability.

As the ship was heeled over, a sudden squall struck, causing water to rush in through the open gun ports. The crew attempted to right the ship and close the ports, but it was too late. The influx of water caused the ship to list heavily, and within minutes, the Royal George capsized and sank. The rapidity of the disaster left little time for those on board to escape, and the loss of life was staggering. Estimates suggest that as many as 900 people perished, including sailors, dockyard workers, and civilians, many of whom were family members visiting the ship.

The sinking of the Royal George was a profound tragedy, deeply affecting the British public and the Royal Navy. The scale of the loss, both in terms of human lives and naval power, was unprecedented. In the immediate aftermath, efforts were made to rescue survivors and recover bodies, but the depth of the water and the chaotic scene made these tasks extremely difficult. The disaster underscored the dangers of naval operations and the ever-present risks faced by those who served at sea.

The loss of the Royal George prompted an official inquiry, which sought to determine the causes of the disaster and assign responsibility. The inquiry concluded that the primary cause was the improper handling of the ship during the maintenance operation. The decision to heel the ship over with the lower gun ports open was identified as a critical error, compounded by the failure to take adequate precautions against sudden weather changes. The inquiry also highlighted deficiencies in the ship's design and maintenance practices, leading to calls for improved safety measures and stricter protocols for such operations.

In the years following the disaster, several attempts were made to salvage the wreck of the Royal George. The wreck lay in relatively shallow water, making it a potential hazard to navigation in the busy waters of the Solent. Early salvage efforts focused on recovering valuable materials and the ship's armaments, but these operations were hampered by the technology and techniques available at the time. It wasn't until the 1830s that significant progress was made, with the development of new diving equipment and salvage methods.

One of the most notable salvage operations was led by John Deane and Charles Deane, pioneers in the field of diving and underwater salvage. Using their newly invented diving apparatus, they were able to explore the wreck more thoroughly and recover additional artifacts and materials. Their work laid the groundwork for future underwater salvage operations and contributed to the development of modern diving techniques. The Deane brothers' efforts were instrumental in clearing the wreck site and ensuring safer navigation in the area.

The sinking of the Royal George also inspired various memorials and commemorations. One of the most prominent is the memorial in Portsmouth, erected in 1783, which stands as a poignant reminder of the tragedy and honors those who lost their lives. The inscription on the memorial highlights the bravery and sacrifice of the ship's crew, as well as the civilian casualties, ensuring that their memory endures. Additionally, the disaster has been the subject of numerous historical studies, books, and even poetry, reflecting its lasting impact on British naval history and collective memory.

The story of the Royal George serves as a testament to the perils of naval warfare and the importance of vigilance and safety in maritime operations. It also underscores the human cost of naval disasters, with the loss of so many lives resonating through the centuries. The lessons learned from the sinking contributed to advancements in naval architecture, safety protocols, and salvage techniques, helping to improve the safety and effectiveness of subsequent generations of warships and their crews.

In the broader context of British naval history, the Royal George represents both the zenith of 18th-century naval power and the vulnerabilities that even the mightiest ships faced. Her career and tragic end encapsulate the triumphs and tribulations of the Age of Sail, a period marked by exploration, conflict, and technological innovation. The Royal George's legacy is one of bravery, sacrifice, and the relentless pursuit of excellence in the face of daunting challenges, reflecting the indomitable spirit of those who served aboard her and in the Royal Navy as a whole.

The Royal George's story also highlights the evolution of maritime practices and the continuous quest for improvement in ship design and safety. The disaster prompted critical reflections and reforms within the Royal Navy, leading to better training for crews, more rigorous maintenance procedures, and advancements in ship construction. These changes not only honored the memory of those lost but also contributed to the enhanced safety and efficiency of naval operations in the years that followed.

Today, the legacy of the HMS Royal George lives on in the annals of naval history and in the ongoing efforts to preserve and study maritime heritage. The shipwreck and its story continue to captivate historians, archaeologists, and the public, offering valuable insights into the past and serving as a powerful reminder of the enduring challenges and risks faced by those who go to sea. The Royal George remains a symbol of the courage and resilience of the Royal Navy, a testament to the human spirit's ability to endure and overcome even the most tragic of circumstances.

# Chapter 24: MV Derbyshire

The MV Derbyshire was a British bulk carrier that met a tragic fate in September 1980, becoming the largest British-flagged ship ever to have been lost at sea. Built by Swan Hunter Shipbuilders in Newcastle upon Tyne and launched in 1976, the Derbyshire was a massive vessel, measuring 294 meters in length and 44.8 meters in width, with a deadweight tonnage of 169,044 tons. Designed primarily for carrying iron ore and other bulk cargo, she was a symbol of the industrial might and advanced maritime engineering of the time. However, her catastrophic loss would raise profound questions about ship design, construction, and safety regulations in the maritime industry.

The Derbyshire embarked on her final voyage on July 11, 1980, from Sept-Îles, Quebec, Canada, bound for Kawasaki, Japan, carrying a cargo of 157,446 tonnes of iron ore. The ship was manned by a crew of 42, including two wives of crew members, bringing the total number of people on board to 44. Commanded by Captain Geoffrey Underhill, an experienced mariner, the Derbyshire was expected to complete its trans-Pacific journey without incident, a routine voyage for a vessel of her class and purpose.

As the Derbyshire approached the western Pacific, it encountered Typhoon Orchid, a powerful storm system that intensified rapidly as it moved across the ocean. On September 9, 1980, the ship was last heard from when it sent routine weather reports indicating the presence of rough seas and increasing winds. Soon after, the Derbyshire and its crew vanished without a trace. When the ship failed to arrive in Japan, search and rescue operations were initiated, but no survivors or debris were found in the immediate aftermath. The ship was officially declared lost, marking the beginning of a long and painful quest for answers by the families of those on board.

The disappearance of the Derbyshire was a significant mystery that baffled maritime experts and investigators for years. Initial theories ranged from catastrophic structural failure to human error, but without concrete evidence, these remained speculative. The loss was particularly poignant for the families of the crew, who were left with unanswered questions and a profound sense of loss. The maritime community was also deeply affected, as the Derbyshire's disappearance highlighted potential vulnerabilities in ship design and operational practices.

In the years following the loss, the Derbyshire Families Association (DFA) was formed, driven by the determination of the relatives to uncover the truth about what happened to their loved ones. They tirelessly campaigned for a thorough investigation into the ship's disappearance, seeking to ensure that no similar tragedies would occur in the future. Their efforts were instrumental in bringing about several inquiries and studies aimed at understanding the circumstances surrounding the loss of the Derbyshire.

In 1994, a significant breakthrough occurred when the wreck of the Derbyshire was located at a depth of approximately 4,200 meters (13,780 feet) in the South China Sea, about 370 kilometers south of Japan. This discovery was made possible by the use of advanced underwater search technology, including remotely operated vehicles (ROVs) and deep-sea submersibles. The wreck site revealed that the ship had broken into two main sections, with debris scattered over a wide area, suggesting a violent and catastrophic failure.

Subsequent investigations, including a detailed survey of the wreck, provided crucial insights into the cause of the disaster. The findings indicated that the Derbyshire had succumbed to structural failure induced by the extreme conditions of Typhoon Orchid. The investigation revealed that the hatch covers on the ship's main deck, which were designed to protect the cargo holds from the ingress of seawater, had been compromised. The storm's immense force had caused these covers to fail, allowing water to flood the holds.

As the ship's holds filled with water, the Derbyshire's stability and buoyancy were severely compromised. The increasing weight of the waterlogged cargo, combined with the relentless pounding of the storm, led to progressive structural failure. The ship's hull and internal structures could not withstand the immense pressures and stresses, resulting in the vessel breaking apart and sinking rapidly. The investigation concluded that poor design and construction practices, inadequate maintenance, and a lack of sufficient safety regulations had contributed to the disaster.

The findings from the Derbyshire investigation had far-reaching implications for the maritime industry. They highlighted the need for improved design standards and construction practices for bulk carriers, particularly concerning the strength and integrity of hatch covers and other critical structures. The investigation also underscored the importance of rigorous maintenance and inspection regimes to ensure that vessels could withstand the harsh conditions encountered at sea.

As a result of the Derbyshire disaster, several important changes were implemented in the maritime industry. The International Maritime Organization (IMO) introduced stricter regulations and guidelines for the construction and maintenance of bulk carriers, aimed at enhancing their safety and survivability. These included more stringent standards for hatch cover strength, hull integrity, and the use of advanced materials and construction techniques to improve the overall robustness of ships.

The legacy of the Derbyshire also extends to the realm of marine safety culture and practices. The disaster underscored the need for better training and awareness among seafarers regarding the potential risks and challenges associated with their work. It prompted the development of enhanced safety protocols and emergency response procedures, aimed at ensuring that crews were better prepared to handle extreme weather conditions and other hazards at sea.

The tireless efforts of the Derbyshire Families Association played a crucial role in bringing about these changes. Their advocacy and persistence ensured that the lessons learned from the tragedy were not forgotten and that meaningful improvements were made to prevent similar incidents in the future. The DFA's work stands as a testament to the power of collective action and the importance of holding the maritime industry accountable for the safety and well-being of those who work at sea.

Today, the story of the MV Derbyshire serves as a poignant reminder of the risks and challenges inherent in maritime operations. It highlights the critical importance of rigorous safety standards, robust design and construction practices, and ongoing vigilance to protect the lives of seafarers and the integrity of the ships on which they depend. The disaster also underscores the human dimension of maritime tragedies, reminding us of the families and communities that are profoundly affected by such events.

In commemorating the MV Derbyshire and those who lost their lives in the disaster, we are reminded of the enduring need to prioritize safety and innovation in the maritime industry. The lessons learned from the Derbyshire continue to inform and inspire efforts to enhance maritime safety, ensuring that the sacrifices of those on board were not in vain and that future generations of seafarers can navigate the world's oceans with greater confidence and security.

# Chapter 25: USS Scorpion

The USS Scorpion (SSN-589) was a Skipjack-class nuclear-powered submarine in the United States Navy, launched on December 29, 1959. Commissioned in July 1960, the Scorpion was part of a fleet designed during the Cold War to maintain American naval superiority, particularly in terms of underwater capabilities. The submarine was built by the Electric Boat Division of General Dynamics in Groton, Connecticut, and was one of the fastest and most advanced submarines of its time, capable of reaching speeds in excess of 30 knots (about 35 mph) while submerged.

The Scorpion's operational history included numerous patrols and missions aimed at gathering intelligence on Soviet naval activities and ensuring American dominance in undersea warfare. These missions were typically highly classified, reflecting the intense strategic rivalry between the United States and the Soviet Union during this period. The Scorpion was equipped with advanced sonar systems, sophisticated torpedoes, and a nuclear reactor that allowed it to remain submerged for extended periods, making it a formidable opponent in naval warfare.

In the spring of 1968, the Scorpion was deployed on a routine operational patrol in the North Atlantic. After completing this mission, she was ordered to return to her home port in Norfolk, Virginia. The last known communication from the submarine was on May 21, 1968, when she reported her position about 50 miles south of the Azores. The message indicated that everything was normal aboard the vessel. However, this would be the last time anyone heard from the Scorpion.

When the submarine failed to arrive in Norfolk as scheduled on May 27, a search and rescue operation was launched. For days, the Navy scoured the North Atlantic for any sign of the missing submarine, but no immediate evidence of the Scorpion or her crew could be found. On June 5, the Navy declared the Scorpion and her 99 crew members lost, marking one of the most mysterious and tragic incidents in the history of the US Navy.

In October 1968, the Navy's oceanographic research ship Mizar located the wreckage of the Scorpion at a depth of about 11,000 feet (3,353 meters) on the floor of the Atlantic Ocean, approximately 400 miles southwest of the Azores. The submarine was found in several pieces, with the hull split into two main sections, indicating a catastrophic event had occurred. The exact cause of the sinking, however, remained a matter of speculation and investigation.

Several theories emerged to explain the sudden loss of the Scorpion. One of the earliest theories suggested a mechanical failure or structural issue, such as a problem with the submarine's nuclear reactor or its hull integrity. Another theory proposed that an accidental explosion of one of the Scorpion's own torpedoes could have caused the disaster. This theory was supported by the fact that the submarine had experienced issues with its torpedo batteries overheating in the past.

The possibility of an external attack, such as a collision with a Soviet submarine or a torpedo strike, was also considered, given the Cold War context. However, there was no concrete evidence to support this theory, and both the United States and the Soviet Union denied any involvement in the incident. The Navy conducted extensive investigations, including a review of acoustic data and an examination of the wreckage, but no definitive conclusion was reached.

In the 1990s, the Navy declassified many of the documents related to the Scorpion's loss, leading to renewed interest and further analysis by independent researchers and former naval personnel. One of the most compelling theories to emerge from these efforts involved a malfunction of the Mark 37 torpedoes carried by the Scorpion. According to this theory, an internal torpedo battery explosion may have occurred, causing the torpedo to detonate within the submarine's torpedo room. This explosion would have led to a catastrophic breach of the hull and the rapid flooding of the vessel.

Despite the extensive investigations and various theories, the precise cause of the Scorpion's sinking remains a mystery. The loss of the submarine had a profound impact on the US Navy and the families of the crew members. It highlighted the inherent dangers of submarine operations and the potential vulnerabilities of even the most advanced naval vessels.

The Scorpion's sinking also had significant implications for submarine design and safety protocols. In the aftermath of the disaster, the Navy implemented a series of improvements aimed at enhancing the safety and reliability of its submarine fleet. These included more rigorous maintenance procedures, better training for submarine crews, and the development of more reliable and safer torpedo systems. The Navy also increased its investment in submarine rescue and salvage technologies to improve its ability to respond to future incidents.

The legacy of the Scorpion lives on as a symbol of the risks and sacrifices associated with submarine service. The submarine community continues to honor the memory of the Scorpion's crew through memorials and commemorative events. The National Museum of the United States Navy in Washington, D.C., features exhibits dedicated to the Scorpion, preserving the history and legacy of this tragic incident for future generations.

The story of the USS Scorpion also serves as a reminder of the intense geopolitical tensions of the Cold War era. The submarine's missions and ultimate fate were shaped by the broader context of the US-Soviet rivalry, reflecting the high-stakes nature of underwater warfare and intelligence gathering during this period. The Scorpion's loss underscores the strategic importance of submarines in national defense and the critical role they played in maintaining the balance of power during the Cold War.

In the years since the Scorpion's sinking, the quest for answers has continued, driven by advances in underwater exploration technology and the enduring determination of the families and colleagues of the lost crew. Organizations such as the US Navy's Underwater Archaeology Branch and independent research groups have conducted further surveys of the wreck site, seeking to gather more data and piece together the final moments of the submarine.

Despite the passage of time, the mystery of the USS Scorpion remains a compelling and poignant chapter in naval history. The submarine's story is a testament to the bravery and dedication of the men who served aboard her, as well as the broader challenges and dangers faced by submariners. It also serves as a sobering reminder of the need for continuous vigilance, innovation, and improvement in submarine design and operations to ensure the safety of those who serve beneath the waves.

Today, the memory of the USS Scorpion and her crew is honored not only by the Navy but also by the wider community of submariners and naval enthusiasts. Memorials and plaques dedicated to the Scorpion can be found at various naval bases and institutions, serving as lasting tributes to the sacrifice and service of the lost submariners. The story of the Scorpion continues to be taught in naval training programs, ensuring that the lessons learned from this tragedy are passed on to future generations of submariners.

# Chapter 26: MS al-Salam Boccaccio 98

The MS al-Salam Boccaccio 98 was an Egyptian roll-on/roll-off (ro-ro) ferry that sank in the Red Sea on February 3, 2006, resulting in the tragic loss of over 1,000 lives. This disaster remains one of the deadliest maritime incidents in recent history, highlighting critical issues in maritime safety, ship design, and regulatory oversight. The ferry's sinking exposed significant shortcomings in emergency preparedness, crew training, and the enforcement of safety standards, sparking widespread outrage and calls for reforms in the global shipping industry.

The MS al-Salam Boccaccio 98 was originally built in 1970 in Italy by the Società Italiana Ernesto Breda shipyard. The ferry was part of the al-Salam Maritime Transport fleet, a company that operated several vessels between Egypt and Saudi Arabia, primarily catering to the large number of Egyptian migrant workers traveling to and from the Gulf region. At 130 meters in length and capable of carrying over 1,400 passengers and crew, along with vehicles and cargo, the al-Salam Boccaccio 98 was a vital link for many travelers in the region.

On the fateful night of February 2, 2006, the ferry departed from the Saudi port of Duba, bound for Safaga, Egypt, on the opposite shore of the Red Sea. Onboard were 1,312 passengers, mostly Egyptian workers returning home, and a crew of 104. Additionally, the ferry was carrying vehicles and cargo. The weather conditions were initially reported as clear, but as the voyage progressed, the ship encountered strong winds and rough seas.

Trouble began shortly after departure when a fire broke out in the engine room, reportedly due to a short circuit. Despite the crew's efforts to extinguish the fire, it quickly spread and compromised the vessel's stability. The situation worsened as the ferry began taking on water, a problem exacerbated by the design of ro-ro ferries, which have large open vehicle decks that can flood rapidly. The ferry's design, which includes large ramps and doors for vehicles, can make it particularly vulnerable to flooding if the hull is breached or if water enters the vehicle decks.

As the fire continued to rage, the crew struggled to manage the growing emergency. Passengers were largely left uninformed about the severity of the situation, contributing to panic and confusion. Reports from survivors indicate that there was a significant delay in issuing evacuation orders, and when the orders were finally given, the evacuation process was chaotic. Lifeboats and life rafts were not deployed effectively, and many passengers found themselves without proper life jackets.

The captain and some senior officers were later criticized for abandoning the ship early in the evacuation process. This action left many passengers without leadership during the critical moments of the disaster. The lack of effective communication and coordination further hindered rescue efforts. As the situation deteriorated, the ferry listed heavily to one side before capsizing and sinking approximately 60 miles off the Egyptian coast.

The response to the sinking was slow and disorganized. It took several hours before rescue operations were fully mobilized. The first rescuers to arrive at the scene were local fishermen, followed by official rescue vessels and helicopters. By the time help arrived, many passengers had already succumbed to the cold waters of the Red Sea. Of the more than 1,400 people onboard, only 388 survived. The bodies of many victims were never recovered, and the exact number of casualties remains uncertain.

In the aftermath of the disaster, investigations were launched to determine the cause of the fire and the factors that led to the high death toll. The Egyptian government, along with international maritime organizations, scrutinized the actions of the ship's crew, the ferry's design, and the safety standards of the al-Salam Maritime Transport Company. It was revealed that the al-Salam Boccaccio 98 had been involved in previous incidents, including a collision in 1999 that raised concerns about its seaworthiness.

One of the key findings was that the ferry's design made it particularly susceptible to capsizing once water began to enter the vehicle decks. Ro-ro ferries, by their nature, have large, undivided spaces that can quickly fill with water, leading to rapid loss of stability. The investigation also pointed to inadequate maintenance and safety procedures onboard. Firefighting equipment was found to be insufficient, and the crew was not adequately trained to handle such emergencies.

The disaster highlighted significant gaps in maritime safety regulations and enforcement. It was found that the ferry had not undergone rigorous safety inspections, and there were questions about whether it met the international standards set by the International Maritime Organization (IMO). The lack of stringent oversight and the failure to enforce existing safety regulations were major factors contributing to the disaster.

The Egyptian government faced intense criticism for its handling of the disaster and the perceived lack of transparency in the investigation. Families of the victims and survivors accused officials of negligence and demanded accountability. The tragedy also brought attention to the broader issue of safety standards in the global shipping industry, particularly for older vessels operating in less regulated waters.

In response to the disaster, several measures were proposed and implemented to improve maritime safety. The IMO reviewed and updated its safety guidelines for passenger ships, especially ro-ro ferries, emphasizing the need for better fire prevention and control measures, improved stability standards, and more effective emergency response protocols. There was also a push for stricter enforcement of safety inspections and certification processes to ensure that ships meet the required standards before being allowed to operate.

The sinking of the MS al-Salam Boccaccio 98 remains a poignant reminder of the critical importance of maritime safety and the need for continuous vigilance and improvement in the industry. The disaster not only resulted in a tragic loss of life but also exposed systemic issues that required urgent attention and reform. While the measures taken in the wake of the tragedy have improved safety standards, the legacy of the al-Salam Boccaccio 98 serves as a stark warning of the consequences of complacency and neglect in maritime operations.

The story of the MS al-Salam Boccaccio 98 is also a testament to the resilience and courage of the survivors and the families of the victims. Their efforts to seek justice and accountability have been instrumental in driving changes that aim to prevent similar disasters in the future. The tragedy underscores the human cost of failures in safety and regulation, and the ongoing need to prioritize the well-being of those who travel and work at sea.

Today, the legacy of the al-Salam Boccaccio 98 continues to influence maritime safety practices and policies. The lessons learned from the disaster have contributed to a greater awareness of the unique risks associated with ro-ro ferries and the importance of rigorous safety standards. As the maritime industry evolves, the memory of those who perished in the Red Sea serves as a powerful reminder of the need for constant vigilance and improvement in the pursuit of safer seas.

# Chapter 27: RMS Queen Mary

The RMS Queen Mary, a magnificent British ocean liner built by John Brown & Company in Clydebank, Scotland, embarked on its maiden voyage on May 27, 1936. Named after Mary of Teck, the wife of King George V, the Queen Mary was celebrated for its luxurious accommodations and speed, quickly becoming one of the most iconic ships of its time. However, it was during the years 1939 to 1945, during World War II, that the Queen Mary's role dramatically shifted from a symbol of opulence to a critical component of the Allied war effort.

As the war escalated, the Queen Mary was requisitioned by the British government for service as a troopship. The ship underwent a significant transformation to meet its new role, painted in a dull grey color for camouflage and stripped of its lavish interior to accommodate thousands of troops. The Queen Mary was nicknamed the "Grey Ghost" due to its new appearance and speed, which made it an elusive target for enemy submarines. This speed was one of its most valuable assets, allowing it to outrun potential threats in the treacherous waters of the Atlantic Ocean.

The Queen Mary's wartime service began in earnest in March 1940. It was tasked with transporting Australian and New Zealand troops to the United Kingdom, a journey that marked the beginning of numerous transoceanic voyages that would see the ship crisscrossing the globe. The ship's capacity was pushed to its limits, with reports indicating that it sometimes carried as many as 16,000 soldiers at a time. This was a far cry from its peacetime capacity of around 2,100 passengers, highlighting the scale of the modifications made to the ship.

One of the Queen Mary's most notable contributions came in 1942 during Operation Bolero, the buildup of U.S. forces in the United Kingdom in preparation for the Allied invasion of Europe. The ship played a crucial role in transporting American troops across the

Atlantic. On one notable voyage in July 1943, the Queen Mary set a record by carrying 15,740 troops and 943 crew members, a record for the most people ever transported on a single voyage.

The Queen Mary's speed and capacity were not its only notable features; its service was also marked by several dramatic incidents. One of the most tragic occurred on October 2, 1942, when the Queen Mary collided with the HMS Curacoa, a British light cruiser, off the coast of Ireland. The Curacoa was sliced in two, and over 300 lives were lost. The Queen Mary, adhering to wartime protocols, could not stop to assist survivors due to the threat of U-boat attacks, a decision that underscored the harsh realities of wartime operations.

The ship's wartime service was not limited to the Atlantic. The Queen Mary also voyaged to the Middle East, India, and Australia, transporting troops to various theaters of war. Each journey posed its own set of challenges, from navigating mine-infested waters to dealing with the threat of air attacks. Despite these dangers, the Queen Mary remained unscathed throughout the war, a testament to the ship's construction and the skill of its crew.

In addition to its transportation duties, the Queen Mary also served as a venue for important wartime conferences. One of the most significant was the meeting between President Franklin D. Roosevelt and British Prime Minister Winston Churchill in 1941. Held on board the Queen Mary, this meeting helped solidify the Anglo-American alliance and coordinate their strategies for the war effort. Such gatherings highlighted the ship's role not just as a transporter but as a floating headquarters for high-level diplomatic and military discussions.

The end of World War II did not immediately mark the end of the Queen Mary's military service. Following the cessation of hostilities in Europe, the ship was involved in repatriating American troops. This phase, known as "Operation Magic Carpet," saw the Queen Mary and other liners working tirelessly to bring millions of soldiers back to their home countries. These voyages were filled with emotional reunions and the promise of peace after years of conflict.

By the end of 1946, the Queen Mary had completed its final troopship duties and was released from military service. The ship returned to its builders for a refit to restore it to its former glory as a luxury ocean liner. This extensive refurbishment included reinstallation of its opulent interiors, modernization of its facilities, and the removal of the wartime gray paint. On July 31, 1947, the Queen Mary resumed regular transatlantic passenger service, sailing from Southampton to New York with a renewed sense of purpose.

The legacy of the Queen Mary's wartime service is multifaceted. It highlights the versatility and resilience of the ship and its crew, capable of adapting to the harsh demands of war while maintaining a commitment to excellence. The ship's ability to carry an unprecedented number of troops safely across hostile waters played a crucial role in the Allied war effort, and its participation in key wartime events underscored its strategic importance.

Today, the Queen Mary is preserved as a museum ship and hotel in Long Beach, California. Visitors can explore its rich history, from its luxurious beginnings to its heroic wartime service. The stories of those who sailed on the Queen Mary during World War II continue to captivate and inspire, serving as a poignant reminder of the sacrifices made and the resilience demonstrated during one of the most challenging periods in modern history. The transformation of the Queen Mary from a symbol of peacetime luxury to a vital wartime asset is a testament to the adaptability and endurance of this remarkable ship, ensuring its place in the annals of maritime history.

# Chapter 28: SS Californian

The SS Californian, a British Leyland Line steamship built by the Caledon Shipbuilding & Engineering Company of Dundee, Scotland, is most famously associated with the RMS Titanic disaster in 1912. Launched in November 1901, the Californian was primarily used for passenger and cargo services between the United Kingdom and the Mediterranean. Its routine service was largely uneventful until the night of April 14-15, 1912, when it became entangled in one of the greatest maritime tragedies of the 20th century.

On April 14, 1912, the Californian, commanded by Captain Stanley Lord, was en route from London to Boston, laden with a cargo of cotton and wool, as well as a relatively small number of passengers. As evening fell, the ship entered a field of drifting icebergs in the North Atlantic. Concerned about the potential dangers, Captain Lord decided to halt the Californian's progress for the night, opting to remain stationary until conditions improved. At around 10:30 p.m., the ship's wireless operator, Cyril F. Evans, sent out a warning to nearby vessels about the ice, a message that was received by the RMS Titanic, then on its maiden voyage from Southampton to New York.

The Titanic's wireless operators, Jack Phillips and Harold Bride, were overwhelmed with passenger messages and responded curtly to the Californian's ice warning, telling Evans to "shut up" as they were busy. Undeterred, the Californian's crew maintained their vigil, with the ship's officers keeping a sharp lookout for any signs of distress or navigational hazards. By 11:40 p.m., the Titanic struck an iceberg, and its fate was sealed. Despite the collision, it took some time before the full gravity of the situation was realized on board the Titanic.

As the Titanic's distress calls began in earnest around 12:15 a.m., the Californian's wireless operator had already gone to bed, as the ship's wireless was typically turned off at night to conserve energy and because it was not common practice to maintain continuous wireless watch outside of scheduled times. This decision would later become a point of intense scrutiny and controversy. On the bridge of the Californian, Second Officer Herbert Stone and Apprentice Officer James Gibson noticed unusual lights and rockets in the distance around 12:45 a.m., but failed to interpret these as distress signals immediately. Despite reporting their observations to Captain Lord, who was resting in the chart room, no decisive action was taken to investigate further or to wake the wireless operator.

As the Titanic sank, launching distress rockets and sending frantic SOS messages, the Californian remained stationary. The exact distance between the two ships has been debated, but estimates suggest it was between five and nineteen miles. The Californian's inaction has been attributed to several factors, including miscommunication among its crew, the assumption that the rockets were not distress signals, and a possible misunderstanding of the ship's location relative to the Titanic.

In the aftermath of the disaster, the Californian's role—or lack thereof—became a focal point of multiple inquiries. The British and American investigations both scrutinized Captain Lord's decisions and the crew's actions. The British Wreck Commissioner's inquiry, led by Lord Mersey, harshly criticized Captain Lord for failing to respond to the distress signals and for not making a more concerted effort to establish communication with the nearby ship. The inquiry concluded that the Californian was much closer to the Titanic than Captain Lord had claimed, and that had he acted promptly, many lives could have been saved. The American inquiry, chaired by Senator William Alden Smith, similarly condemned the inaction of the Californian's crew, further tarnishing Captain Lord's reputation.

Captain Lord and his supporters argued in defense of his actions, suggesting that the rockets observed could not have been distress signals due to their color and timing, and that the Californian's position had been misunderstood. Despite these arguments, public opinion and official verdicts were largely unforgiving, and Captain

Lord's career suffered greatly. The stigma of the Californian's perceived failure to assist the Titanic persisted, overshadowing any other aspects of the ship's service.

After the inquiries, the SS Californian continued to operate under the Leyland Line. However, the shadow of the Titanic disaster loomed large over its subsequent voyages. The ship changed hands several times, serving various shipping lines before the outbreak of World War I. In 1915, while en route from Salonika to Marseilles with a cargo of cotton, the Californian was torpedoed and sunk by the German submarine U-35. All crew members were safely evacuated before the ship sank, marking a relatively undramatic end to a vessel forever linked with one of history's most infamous maritime tragedies.

The legacy of the SS Californian is a complex one. While it was an unremarkable vessel in terms of design and service, its inaction on the night of April 14-15, 1912, has ensured its place in history. The incident has been the subject of extensive analysis, debate, and reinterpretation over the years, with some historians arguing that the Californian was unfairly judged, while others maintain that it represents a cautionary tale about the importance of vigilance and responsiveness at sea. The story of the Californian is a reminder of how crucial decisions—or the lack thereof—can have far-reaching consequences, and it continues to be studied as a case of maritime ethics, command responsibility, and the human elements that contribute to disaster.

# Chapter 29: SS Central America

The SS Central America, often referred to as the "Ship of Gold," was a 280-foot sidewheel steamer that played a significant role in the mid-19th century maritime history of the United States. Built in 1852 by William H. Webb in New York City, it was originally named the SS George Law after a prominent financier and later renamed SS Central America. The ship was part of the United States Mail Steamship Company, which provided transportation and mail services between the East Coast and the isthmus of Panama, a key route during the California Gold Rush.

The Central America was a state-of-the-art vessel for its time, designed for both speed and comfort. It featured a large paddle wheel on each side of its hull, powered by a steam engine, and was equipped with luxurious accommodations for its passengers. The ship's primary route involved transporting passengers and gold from the California Gold Rush to the East Coast. The gold was initially transported by land across the isthmus of Panama, then loaded onto ships like the Central America for the voyage to New York.

In September 1857, the Central America embarked on what would be its final voyage. The ship departed from the port of Colón, Panama, on September 3, 1857, under the command of Captain William Lewis Herndon, a respected naval officer and explorer. On board were nearly 600 passengers and crew, along with an estimated three tons of gold, valued at approximately $8 million at the time—a fortune in today's currency.

As the Central America sailed northward, it encountered a series of increasingly severe weather conditions. By September 9, the ship was off the coast of the Carolinas when it ran into a catastrophic hurricane. The storm battered the Central America with high winds and massive waves, causing significant damage to the vessel. Despite the crew's best efforts to manage the situation, including attempts to pump water out of the ship and jettison cargo to lighten the load, the damage proved too extensive.

By September 11, the ship was in dire straits. The hurricane had rendered the paddle wheels inoperable and flooded the engine room, leaving the Central America dead in the water. The relentless waves continued to pound the ship, and it began to sink. Captain Herndon, exhibiting remarkable leadership and courage, organized the evacuation efforts, prioritizing women and children for the lifeboats. However, the available lifeboats were insufficient for the number of passengers on board.

As the situation grew more desperate, Captain Herndon ordered distress signals to be sent out, hoping for rescue by any nearby ships. Some vessels did respond, but the violent sea conditions made rescue operations extremely perilous. Ultimately, only a fraction of those on board were saved by passing ships, including the Norwegian bark Ellen, which managed to rescue 49 survivors. Tragically, the Central America sank on September 12, 1857, taking with it approximately 425 lives and the vast treasure it carried.

The sinking of the SS Central America had far-reaching consequences beyond the immediate loss of life and treasure. The ship's cargo of gold was a significant portion of the wealth flowing from California to the Eastern financial markets. Its loss contributed to the Panic of 1857, a financial crisis that saw numerous banks and businesses fail across the United States. The sudden scarcity of gold and the subsequent tightening of credit had a ripple effect throughout the economy, exacerbating an already volatile financial situation.

The heroism of Captain Herndon became legendary. Survivors recounted his calm and resolute demeanor in the face of disaster, as he coordinated the evacuation and ultimately went down with his ship. In recognition of his bravery, the U.S. Navy named a new destroyer, USS Herndon, in his honor, and a monument was erected at the United States Naval Academy to commemorate his sacrifice.

For over a century, the wreck of the SS Central America lay undisturbed on the ocean floor. The exact location remained a mystery until the 1980s when a team led by maritime engineer and treasure hunter Tommy Thompson set out to locate and recover the ship's cargo. Using advanced technology, including remotely operated underwater vehicles (ROVs), Thompson's team successfully located the wreck in 1987, approximately 160 miles off the coast of South Carolina at a depth of 7,200 feet.

The discovery of the Central America and its cargo sparked immense excitement and legal battles. The recovery operation yielded a staggering amount of gold, including coins, bars, and nuggets, as well as other artifacts from the ship. The total value of the recovered treasure was estimated to be in the hundreds of millions of dollars, making it one of the most valuable shipwreck discoveries in history.

However, the recovery operation also led to extensive legal disputes over the ownership of the treasure. Various insurance companies, which had paid out claims following the ship's sinking, claimed rights to the gold, leading to a protracted legal battle that lasted for years. Eventually, a settlement was reached, and the treasure was divided among the parties involved.

The recovered artifacts from the Central America provided a remarkable glimpse into mid-19th century life and the history of the California Gold Rush. Items recovered included personal belongings of passengers, tools, and even clothing, preserved by the cold, deep-sea environment. These artifacts have been displayed in museums and exhibitions, allowing the public to connect with this dramatic chapter in American history.

The story of the SS Central America is a multifaceted tale of adventure, tragedy, and discovery. It highlights the perilous nature of sea travel in the 19th century, the impact of the California Gold Rush on the American economy, and the enduring human fascination with sunken treasure. The ship's sinking remains one of the most significant maritime disasters of its time, and the subsequent recovery of its treasure has ensured that the legacy of the Central America continues to captivate the imagination of people around the world.

# Chapter 30: Vasa

The Vasa, a Swedish warship constructed in the early 17th century, is one of the most famous maritime disasters in history, not because of an encounter with an enemy or natural disaster, but due to a tragic flaw in its design. Commissioned by King Gustavus Adolphus of Sweden, the Vasa was intended to be a symbol of Swedish naval power and technological advancement during a period of intense military conflict in Europe. Its story, encompassing ambitious design, flawed execution, and remarkable preservation, offers a profound insight into naval engineering and the socio-political context of its time.

Construction of the Vasa began in 1626 at the shipyard in Stockholm under the supervision of master shipbuilder Henrik Hybertsson. The ship was part of a broader plan to bolster the Swedish navy, which played a crucial role in the Thirty Years' War. Sweden, under Gustavus Adolphus, was emerging as a significant European power, and the Vasa was to be the crown jewel of its navy, a formidable warship equipped with the latest armaments and designed to project Swedish might.

The Vasa was an impressive vessel by any standard. Measuring approximately 69 meters (226 feet) in length, it was heavily armed with 64 bronze cannons, making it one of the most powerfully armed ships of its era. Its construction incorporated ornate carvings and decorations, reflecting the grandeur and authority of the Swedish monarchy. The ship's design featured two-gun decks, a tall sterncastle, and a high rigging system, all of which contributed to its majestic appearance.

However, the Vasa's design also harbored critical flaws. The ship's construction was rushed due to the pressing demands of war, and there were significant issues with its stability. The Vasa's tall structure and heavy armament made it top-heavy. During the construction phase, Henrik Hybertsson fell ill and was replaced by another master shipbuilder, Hein Jacobsson, who continued the project without fully addressing the stability concerns. There was little time for comprehensive testing or adjustments, and the shipbuilders were under immense pressure to deliver the vessel quickly.

On August 10, 1628, the Vasa was ready for its maiden voyage. The event was a grand affair, attended by numerous dignitaries and citizens who gathered to witness the launch of Sweden's pride. The ship set sail from the Skeppsholmen dockyard in Stockholm harbor with a crew of around 145 sailors and soldiers, along with their families and guests, bringing the total number of people on board to about 150 to 200.

As the Vasa embarked on its voyage, it soon became apparent that something was amiss. A gust of wind filled the ship's sails, causing it to lean precariously to one side. Although it righted itself momentarily, another stronger gust followed, causing the ship to list even further. Water began to pour in through the open gun ports, and within minutes, the Vasa sank to the bottom of Stockholm harbor, less than a mile from its starting point. The disaster resulted in the deaths of at least 30 people, although many managed to swim to safety or were rescued by nearby boats.

The sinking of the Vasa was a national embarrassment for Sweden, a stark contrast to the grandeur and power it was supposed to symbolize. Immediate investigations were launched to determine the cause of the disaster. The inquiries revealed that the ship's instability was well known among the builders and crew, but the pressure to launch the ship on schedule and the lack of a unified command structure contributed to the oversight of these critical issues.

Despite the initial inquiries, no one was held formally accountable for the disaster, and the Vasa soon faded into the depths of Stockholm harbor, largely forgotten by the public. For over three centuries, it lay submerged, preserved by the brackish waters of the Baltic Sea, which inhibited the growth of wood-destroying organisms.

In the late 1950s, interest in the Vasa was rekindled by Anders Franzén, an amateur archaeologist and naval historian who had been researching shipwrecks in the Baltic Sea. Franzén believed that the unique conditions of the Baltic would have preserved the ship remarkably well. His persistence paid off when, in 1956, he located the Vasa's exact resting place. With the assistance of the Swedish navy and various experts, a plan was developed to raise the ship from its watery grave.

The salvage operation began in 1961 and was an enormous technical challenge. The Vasa was carefully lifted in stages using a system of steel cables and pontoons. After nearly 333 years underwater, the ship was brought to the surface, revealing an astonishingly well-preserved relic of the 17th century. The hull was largely intact, along with many of its original features, including the ornate carvings and much of its wooden structure.

Following its recovery, the Vasa underwent extensive conservation efforts to ensure its preservation for future generations. The ship was sprayed with polyethylene glycol, a chemical that helps stabilize waterlogged wood, for many years to replace the water content in the wood with a more stable substance. This process, along with the controlled environment of the Vasa Museum in Stockholm, has helped preserve the ship to an extraordinary degree.

The Vasa Museum, opened in 1990, is now one of Sweden's most popular tourist attractions, drawing visitors from around the world. The museum not only showcases the ship itself but also offers a wealth of information about 17th-century maritime life, shipbuilding techniques, and the historical context of the Vasa's construction and sinking. The museum's exhibits include artifacts recovered from the wreck, such as personal belongings of the passengers and crew, tools, weapons, and even the remains of some of the individuals who perished in the disaster.

The Vasa's story is a poignant reminder of the interplay between ambition and oversight, technological advancement and human error. It provides invaluable insights into the era of its construction, from the political ambitions of Sweden under Gustavus Adolphus to the everyday lives of the people who sailed on such ships. The Vasa also serves as a case study in maritime archaeology and conservation, illustrating how modern techniques can recover and preserve historical artifacts for educational and cultural enrichment.

The Vasa's legacy is multifaceted. It stands as a symbol of Swedish naval history and a testament to the craftsmanship and ambition of the 17th century. At the same time, it is a cautionary tale about the importance of thorough planning and testing in engineering projects. The ship's remarkable preservation and the successful efforts to raise and conserve it have ensured that the Vasa continues to educate and inspire, connecting us with a pivotal moment in maritime history and offering lessons that remain relevant to this day.

# Chapter 31: K-129

The story of the Soviet submarine K-129, which sank in 1968, is a gripping tale of Cold War intrigue, maritime mystery, and advanced underwater technology. This incident, shrouded in secrecy and speculation, offers a fascinating glimpse into the intense rivalry between the superpowers of the era, the Soviet Union and the United States. The events surrounding K-129's final mission, its loss, and the subsequent efforts by the United States to recover its remains, highlight the lengths to which these nations went to gain a strategic advantage.

K-129 was a Project 629A (Golf II-class) ballistic missile submarine of the Soviet Navy. Launched in 1959, this diesel-electric submarine was equipped with three R-21 ballistic missiles and a torpedo armament, designed to be part of the Soviet Union's second-strike nuclear capability. The submarine, like others in its class, represented a crucial component of the Soviet Union's strategy to maintain a credible deterrent against the United States during the height of the Cold War.

In February 1968, K-129 set sail from its base in Kamchatka on what was to be a routine patrol in the Pacific Ocean. The mission was typical of the Cold War-era deployments, intended to maintain a hidden, mobile nuclear strike force that could retaliate in the event of a first strike by the United States. On March 8, 1968, however, K-129 failed to make a scheduled radio check-in, and subsequent attempts to contact the submarine were unsuccessful. By March 11, the Soviet Navy declared the submarine lost, initiating a frantic search operation.

The exact circumstances of K-129's sinking remain a subject of much speculation and debate. Some theories suggest that an internal explosion or mechanical failure could have caused the submarine to sink. Other hypotheses, more conspiratorial in nature, propose that K-129 might have collided with a U.S. submarine or even attempted an unauthorized missile launch that went disastrously wrong. Despite extensive search efforts by the Soviet Navy, the exact location of K-129 remained elusive.

Unbeknownst to the Soviets, the U.S. intelligence community had been monitoring the activities of Soviet submarines closely. The United States had deployed a network of underwater listening devices known as the Sound Surveillance System (SOSUS), which detected acoustic anomalies consistent with the explosion and sinking of a submarine in the North Pacific. Using this data, the U.S. Navy was able to narrow down the possible location of K-129's wreck.

In 1968, a classified U.S. Navy operation, known as Project Azorian (often mistakenly referred to as Project Jennifer), was initiated to locate and potentially recover the sunken submarine. The project was an ambitious and highly secretive effort led by the CIA, with significant input from naval experts and engineers. The goal was to salvage the submarine, or at least parts of it, to gain intelligence on Soviet naval capabilities and missile technology.

To accomplish this, the CIA enlisted the help of billionaire industrialist Howard Hughes, who provided cover for the operation under the guise of a deep-sea mining expedition. Hughes's company, Global Marine Development Inc., constructed a specially designed vessel, the Hughes Glomar Explorer, which was ostensibly built to harvest manganese nodules from the ocean floor. In reality, the ship was equipped with a massive mechanical claw designed to lift the submarine from the depths.

In August 1974, after years of meticulous planning and construction, the Hughes Glomar Explorer set sail for the recovery site, located approximately 1,500 miles northwest of Hawaii, in waters nearly three miles deep. The operation to retrieve K-129 was fraught with challenges, including the extreme depth, the need for precise navigation, and the technical difficulties of lifting a large and fragile object from the ocean floor.

Despite these challenges, the recovery team managed to bring a portion of the submarine to the surface. Reports suggest that the claw successfully grasped part of the submarine, but as it was being lifted, a structural failure caused a large section to break off and fall back to the seabed. The exact contents of the recovered section have been a matter of speculation, but it is believed to have included two nuclear-armed torpedoes, various documents, and possibly the remains of six Soviet sailors.

The secrecy surrounding Project Azorian was maintained for several decades. The United States government did not officially acknowledge the operation, and the details were only revealed gradually through leaks and declassified documents. One of the most significant disclosures came in 1975 when the New York Times published an exposé based on information provided by former CIA personnel, which confirmed the broad outlines of the mission but left many specifics unclear.

The implications of Project Azorian were profound. The successful recovery of even a part of K-129 provided the United States with valuable intelligence on Soviet naval technology and missile systems. It also underscored the extraordinary lengths to which the U.S. was willing to go to gather intelligence during the Cold War. Moreover, the operation demonstrated the potential of deep-sea salvage technology, setting a precedent for future underwater recovery missions.

For the Soviet Union, the loss of K-129 and the subsequent American recovery efforts represented a significant blow. The Soviet Navy had failed to locate and salvage the submarine, and the realization that the United States had not only found but also partially recovered it, was a source of considerable embarrassment and concern. The incident likely intensified the Soviets' efforts to improve the security and survivability of their ballistic missile submarine fleet.

In the years since Project Azorian, various accounts and memoirs have shed additional light on the mission. The CIA declassified a report on the project in 2010, providing further details on the technical and operational challenges faced by the recovery team. These accounts have contributed to a more comprehensive understanding of one of the most ambitious intelligence operations of the Cold War.

The story of K-129 and Project Azorian continues to captivate historians, naval experts, and the public. It represents a remarkable convergence of maritime engineering, intelligence gathering, and geopolitical maneuvering. The legacy of K-129 is a testament to the lengths to which nations will go in the pursuit of strategic advantage and the enduring mysteries of the deep ocean. While many questions about the submarine's final voyage and the exact contents of its recovered section remain unanswered, the tale of K-129 is a powerful reminder of the high stakes and extraordinary efforts that defined the Cold War era.

# Chapter 32: MV Princess of the Stars

The MV Princess of the Stars was a Philippine passenger ferry operated by Sulpicio Lines, which tragically capsized and sank during Typhoon Fengshen on June 21, 2008. This disaster resulted in one of the worst maritime tragedies in Philippine history, with the loss of nearly 800 lives. The sinking highlighted critical issues in maritime safety, regulatory oversight, and emergency response, raising questions about the responsibilities and practices of shipping companies and regulatory bodies in ensuring the safety of sea travelers.

The MV Princess of the Stars was a roll-on/roll-off (RoRo) ferry, a type of vessel designed to carry both passengers and vehicles. Built in 1984 by the Japanese shipyard Onomichi Dockyard Co., the ferry was originally named Ferry Lilac and operated in Japan before being acquired by Sulpicio Lines in 2004. The vessel was 23,824 gross tons, 195 meters long, and capable of carrying 1,992 passengers and crew members along with vehicles and cargo. The Princess of the Stars was one of the largest vessels in the Sulpicio Lines fleet and was a critical component of their inter-island transportation service in the Philippines.

On June 20, 2008, the Princess of the Stars departed from Manila, bound for Cebu City with 862 passengers and crew aboard. The voyage began under the looming threat of Typhoon Fengshen, known locally as Typhoon Frank. Fengshen was a powerful tropical cyclone that had already caused significant damage and fatalities in the Philippines. Despite warnings and the severe weather forecast, the decision was made to proceed with the journey, a decision that would later come under intense scrutiny.

As the ferry made its way through the Sibuyan Sea, it encountered the full force of the typhoon. Fengshen, at its peak intensity, brought winds exceeding 100 miles per hour and generated massive waves, making navigation extremely hazardous. The vessel, unable to withstand the relentless onslaught of the storm, began to take on water. The situation deteriorated rapidly, and the ferry started to list and eventually capsized, capsizing completely and sinking. The final moments of the ship were chaotic, with passengers and crew struggling to find safety as the vessel succumbed to the ocean.

The disaster unfolded quickly, leaving little time for a coordinated evacuation. Many passengers were trapped inside the ship as it tilted and sank, while others were thrown into the tumultuous sea. Rescue operations were severely hampered by the continuing storm, and the first responders were unable to reach the scene until after the typhoon had passed. In the aftermath, rescue teams found the capsized hull of the ferry floating in the water, a grim testament to the tragedy that had occurred.

Of the 862 people on board, only 32 survived. The survivors were rescued from the water or found clinging to debris. Many of the bodies were never recovered, believed to be trapped inside the submerged vessel. The loss of life was staggering, and the disaster prompted widespread grief and outrage across the Philippines and beyond.

The sinking of the Princess of the Stars raised immediate and serious questions about the decisions made by Sulpicio Lines and the regulatory authorities. Critics questioned why the ferry was allowed to sail despite the clear and present danger posed by Typhoon Fengshen. There were calls for a thorough investigation into the practices of the shipping company, the enforcement of maritime safety regulations, and the overall state of the country's maritime industry.

In the aftermath of the disaster, the Philippine government launched an inquiry into the circumstances surrounding the sinking. The investigation focused on several key areas: the decision-making process that led to the ferry's departure, the adequacy of safety measures and emergency protocols on board the vessel, and the role of the regulatory authorities in monitoring and ensuring the safety of maritime operations.

The findings of the inquiry highlighted multiple failures and lapses in judgment. It was revealed that the decision to set sail was made despite clear warnings from the Philippine Atmospheric, Geophysical and Astronomical Services Administration (PAGASA) about the severity of the approaching typhoon. Furthermore, there were questions about whether the ship's crew was adequately trained to handle such extreme conditions and whether the ferry was equipped with sufficient life-saving equipment.

The inquiry also scrutinized the role of the Maritime Industry Authority (MARINA) and the Philippine Coast Guard in enforcing safety regulations. The investigation pointed to systemic issues within these regulatory bodies, including inadequate inspections, insufficient enforcement of safety standards, and a lack of rigorous oversight of the shipping companies operating in Philippine waters.

The disaster also brought to light the troubled history of Sulpicio Lines; a company that had been involved in several previous maritime accidents. Notably, Sulpicio Lines was the operator of the MV Doña Paz, which sank in 1987 after colliding with an oil tanker, resulting in the deadliest peacetime maritime disaster in history with over 4,000 fatalities. The repeated involvement of Sulpicio Lines in such tragedies underscored the need for comprehensive reforms in the maritime industry to prevent future disasters.

In response to the public outcry and the findings of the inquiry, the Philippine government implemented several measures aimed at improving maritime safety. These measures included stricter enforcement of weather advisories, enhanced training programs for ship crews, and more rigorous inspections of vessels. Additionally, there were calls for greater accountability and transparency within the regulatory bodies to ensure that safety standards were upheld consistently.

The disaster also had legal repercussions for Sulpicio Lines. The company faced multiple lawsuits from the families of the victims, seeking compensation for the loss of their loved ones. The legal battles were protracted and complex, involving questions of liability, negligence, and the adequacy of the safety measures in place at the time of the disaster. Ultimately, the company was found liable for the tragedy, and substantial damages were awarded to the victims' families.

Beyond the immediate legal and regulatory responses, the sinking of the Princess of the Stars had a lasting impact on the collective consciousness of the Philippines. The disaster served as a stark reminder of the fragility of life at sea and the critical importance of stringent safety measures in protecting passengers and crew. It also highlighted the broader issues of corruption, complacency, and inadequate infrastructure that plagued the country's maritime industry.

The legacy of the Princess of the Stars disaster is multifaceted. On one hand, it serves as a cautionary tale about the dangers of neglecting safety protocols and the devastating consequences that can result from such oversight. On the other hand, it has catalyzed significant changes in the Philippine maritime industry, leading to improved safety standards and greater awareness of the need for vigilance and accountability in maritime operations.

In the years since the disaster, efforts have continued to ensure that the lessons learned from the sinking of the Princess of the Stars are not forgotten. Maritime safety has become a priority for both the government and private sector, with ongoing initiatives to enhance the training of ship crews, improve vessel maintenance, and strengthen the regulatory framework governing maritime operations.

The story of the MV Princess of the Stars is one of tragedy and loss, but it is also a story of resilience and the enduring human spirit. The families of the victims, the survivors, and the broader maritime community have all played a role in shaping the response to the disaster and ensuring that the memories of those who perished are honored through meaningful action and lasting change.

# Chapter 33: RMS Lancastria

The RMS Lancastria, a British ocean liner operated by the Cunard Line, is remembered for one of the worst maritime disasters in British history. The ship, originally launched in 1920 and initially named Tyrrhenia, was built by William Beardmore and Company in Glasgow. It was later renamed Lancastria in 1924. Designed for transatlantic crossings and accommodating up to 2,200 passengers, the Lancastria played various roles throughout its two-decade career, including serving as a cruise ship. However, its most tragic and significant role came during World War II, when it was requisitioned by the British government as a troopship.

In the spring of 1940, World War II had taken a dire turn for the Allies. Germany's Blitzkrieg tactics had overwhelmed much of Western Europe, and the British Expeditionary Force, along with other Allied troops, found themselves retreating towards the coast of France, seeking evacuation. Operation Dynamo, the famous evacuation of Dunkirk, had successfully rescued a large number of soldiers, but many more remained stranded across various French ports. Operation Aerial was subsequently launched to evacuate British and Allied forces from western France, extending the rescue efforts beyond Dunkirk.

The Lancastria was assigned to this mission. On June 17, 1940, the ship anchored off the coast of Saint-Nazaire, a crucial port on the French Atlantic coast. The port was a scene of chaos, with thousands of soldiers, civilian refugees, and equipment crowding the docks, desperate to escape the advancing German forces. The Lancastria took on as many people as it could, a number that far exceeded its official capacity. Estimates suggest that between 5,000 and 9,000 people were crammed aboard, including military personnel, civilian refugees, and crew members.

As the Lancastria lay at anchor, the situation grew increasingly perilous. Around 3:48 p.m., German aircraft attacked the crowded ship. Junkers Ju 88 bombers, part of the Luftwaffe, launched a devastating assault. The Lancastria was struck by several bombs. One bomb penetrated the cargo hold, where munitions and fuel were stored, causing a massive explosion. The ship quickly began to list to starboard and then capsized, sinking within twenty minutes.

The sinking of the Lancastria resulted in a catastrophic loss of life. Estimates of the number of casualties vary, but it is generally believed that between 3,000 and 5,800 people perished, making it one of the deadliest maritime disasters in history. The exact number of victims is uncertain due to the chaotic circumstances and incomplete passenger records. Many of those who died were trapped inside the ship, unable to escape the rapidly rising waters. Others succumbed to drowning or exposure in the oil-coated sea, which had become a flaming inferno in places due to the spilled fuel.

Survivors faced harrowing conditions. Rescue efforts were hampered by continued attacks from German aircraft, which strafed the water with machine-gun fire, targeting those attempting to flee the sinking ship. Nevertheless, some survivors were picked up by other vessels in the area, including British destroyers and various smaller boats. Their accounts paint a vivid picture of the horror and desperation experienced during those critical moments.

The British government, concerned about the potential impact on public morale, imposed a strict news blackout on the disaster. Prime Minister Winston Churchill ordered that news of the sinking be withheld, stating, "The newspapers have got quite enough disaster for today at least." The fall of France and the dire situation in Europe were already causing great concern, and the government feared that news of the Lancastria disaster would further demoralize the British public. As a result, the tragedy remained largely unknown to the wider world for some time.

The story of the Lancastria gradually emerged through the accounts of survivors and witnesses. In the years that followed, survivors and their families campaigned for recognition of the tragedy and for the memory of those who lost their lives to be honored appropriately. Memorial services were held, and plaques and monuments were erected in various locations, including Saint-Nazaire, Glasgow, and Liverpool, to commemorate the victims.

The sinking of the Lancastria had several significant implications. It highlighted the severe risks faced during wartime evacuations and the immense challenges involved in conducting large-scale rescues under enemy fire. The tragedy also underscored the vulnerability of ships to air attacks, leading to changes in naval tactics and the development of better defenses against aerial threats.

In addition to its immediate impact, the Lancastria disaster had long-term effects on British maritime policy and military strategy. The loss of so many lives emphasized the need for improved safety measures and more effective coordination during evacuations. It also contributed to a greater focus on securing air superiority to protect naval and ground operations, an aspect that became increasingly crucial as the war progressed.

Over the decades, historians and researchers have sought to piece together the full story of the Lancastria. Numerous books, documentaries, and articles have been produced, offering detailed accounts of the ship's final voyage, the attack, and the aftermath. These works have helped to ensure that the memory of the Lancastria and its victims is preserved, providing a valuable historical record of one of the many tragic events of World War II.

In recent years, efforts to commemorate the Lancastria have continued, with various organizations and individuals dedicated to keeping the memory of the disaster alive. Annual memorial services are held, and initiatives to educate the public about the event have been undertaken. The Lancastria Association of Scotland, for example, has played a key role in advocating for recognition and remembrance of the tragedy.

The legacy of the Lancastria disaster extends beyond the immediate context of World War II. It serves as a poignant reminder of the human cost of war and the sacrifices made by countless individuals during times of conflict. The story of the Lancastria also highlights the importance of resilience, remembrance, and the enduring quest for justice and recognition for those who have suffered and died in wartime.

# Chapter 34: SS Camorta

The SS Camorta was a British passenger and cargo steamship operated by the British India Steam Navigation Company, which met a tragic end in 1902. Its story is one of maritime disaster that illustrates the perilous nature of sea travel in the early 20th century, especially in the unpredictable and often treacherous waters of the Bay of Bengal. The Camorta's sinking is a significant historical event, marked by the loss of numerous lives and contributing to an understanding of maritime safety developments.

The SS Camorta was built in 1880 by A. & J. Inglis, a shipbuilding company based in Glasgow, Scotland. It was designed as a passenger and cargo steamer, measuring 75 meters (246 feet) in length, with a beam of 10 meters (33 feet) and a gross tonnage of 1,676 tons. The ship was part of a fleet operated by the British India Steam Navigation Company, a prominent maritime enterprise that provided crucial transport links between British colonies and the mother country. The Camorta primarily served routes connecting ports in India, the Straits Settlements (modern-day Singapore and Malaysia), and Burma (now Myanmar).

The ship was equipped with modern features for its time, including a single screw propeller driven by a compound steam engine, which enabled it to navigate the challenging conditions of the Indian Ocean and the Bay of Bengal. It was capable of carrying a substantial number of passengers and cargo, making it a vital link in the colonial transportation network. The Camorta played an essential role in the movement of people and goods within the British Empire, facilitating economic and social exchanges across vast distances.

On May 6, 1902, the SS Camorta set sail from Rangoon (now Yangon), Burma, bound for Calcutta (now Kolkata), India. The journey was expected to be routine, part of the ship's regular schedule. Onboard were 74 crew members and approximately 650 passengers, mostly Indian laborers and their families, who were traveling for work and other purposes. The weather at the time of departure was reported to be fair, and there were no immediate indications of trouble.

However, as the Camorta steamed into the Bay of Bengal, it encountered one of the most fearsome and deadly forces of nature in the region: a powerful cyclone. The Bay of Bengal is notorious for its cyclonic storms, which can form rapidly and unleash devastating winds and waves. The Camorta soon found itself in the path of such a cyclone, which had intensified into a severe tropical storm by May 11, 1902.

The storm, known as the 1902 Calcutta cyclone, was one of the deadliest in the region's history. With wind speeds estimated to have reached over 100 miles per hour, the cyclone brought massive waves and torrential rain. The ship, not designed to withstand such extreme conditions, was soon overwhelmed by the ferocity of the storm. As the cyclone's full force hit the Camorta, the ship struggled to maintain its course and stability. The crew and passengers faced mounting terror as the vessel was tossed about by the powerful waves.

Eyewitness accounts and subsequent investigations suggest that the ship may have been swamped by the massive waves or capsized due to the violent winds and shifting cargo. The exact sequence of events leading to the sinking remains unclear, as there were no survivors from the disaster to provide a detailed narrative. What is known is that the Camorta was lost with all hands and passengers on board. The total number of fatalities is estimated to be around 750, making it one of the deadliest maritime disasters of its time.

The sinking of the SS Camorta shocked the British maritime community and the public. The loss of so many lives in a single incident highlighted the dangers of sea travel, particularly in regions prone to severe weather conditions. In the aftermath of the disaster, efforts were made to locate the wreck and recover bodies, but the severity of the cyclone and the vast expanse of the Bay of Bengal made these efforts largely unsuccessful. The ship and its passengers were lost to the depths, a somber reminder of the perils faced by those who ventured to sea.

The tragedy of the Camorta had several significant implications. It prompted a re-evaluation of maritime safety practices, particularly concerning the design and operation of passenger ships in regions susceptible to severe weather. The British India Steam Navigation Company, along with other maritime enterprises, began to incorporate more rigorous safety measures, including improved weather forecasting, better ship construction standards, and enhanced training for crew members in emergency procedures.

Furthermore, the disaster underscored the importance of developing more reliable communication systems at sea. At the time, radio technology was still in its infancy, and ships often relied on visual signals and limited wireless telegraphy for communication. The inability to send distress signals effectively hampered rescue efforts and highlighted the need for advancements in maritime communication technology. In the years following the Camorta disaster, significant progress was made in this area, leading to the widespread adoption of wireless radio communication on ships, which greatly improved safety at sea.

The sinking of the Camorta also had a profound impact on the communities affected by the disaster. Many of the passengers were Indian laborers traveling with their families, and their loss was deeply felt in their home regions. The tragedy brought attention to the conditions faced by laborers who traveled by sea, often in overcrowded and under-equipped vessels. This awareness eventually contributed to better regulations and protections for workers traveling long distances by sea.

In historical context, the story of the SS Camorta is a poignant chapter in the broader narrative of maritime history. It illustrates the constant battle between human ingenuity and the forces of nature, a theme that resonates throughout the annals of seafaring. The disaster is a testament to the bravery and resilience of those who venture into the unknown, whether driven by economic necessity, exploration, or the pursuit of new opportunities.

The legacy of the Camorta disaster extends beyond its immediate impact. It serves as a reminder of the inherent risks of maritime travel and the ongoing need to advance safety measures and technology to protect lives at sea. The lessons learned from the tragedy have contributed to the development of modern maritime practices, ensuring that such disasters are less likely to occur in the future.

In the years following the disaster, the memory of the Camorta and its passengers was honored in various ways. Memorials and commemorative events were held to pay tribute to those who lost their lives. These acts of remembrance helped to keep the story of the Camorta alive, ensuring that the sacrifices made on that fateful voyage were not forgotten.

Today, the story of the SS Camorta remains an important part of maritime history, offering valuable insights into the challenges and dangers of sea travel in the early 20th century. It serves as a case study in the complexities of maritime safety, the unpredictability of nature, and the human cost of progress and exploration. The legacy of the Camorta disaster continues to inform and inspire efforts to make sea travel safer and more reliable, honoring the memory of those who perished in one of the most tragic maritime disasters of its time.

# Chapter 35: MV Goya

The story of the MV Goya, a German transport ship sunk in the final days of World War II, is one of the most tragic and harrowing maritime disasters in history. Named after the Spanish painter Francisco Goya, the MV Goya was originally a Norwegian ship built in 1940, later seized by Germany during the war and repurposed as a transport vessel. The ship's sinking on April 16, 1945, led to the loss of thousands of lives, making it one of the deadliest maritime tragedies of the war, and its story is a somber reminder of the human cost of conflict.

The MV Goya was initially constructed as a freighter by Akers Mekaniske Verksted in Oslo, Norway, and launched in 1940. The ship was 146 meters (479 feet) long, with a beam of 17 meters (56 feet), and had a gross tonnage of 5,230 tons. Its design was typical of the freighters of the time, built to carry cargo across the Atlantic. However, with the German occupation of Norway in 1940, the Goya was seized by the Kriegsmarine (the German Navy) and converted into a transport vessel to support the war effort.

Throughout the war, the MV Goya was used primarily for transporting troops and supplies. As the conflict progressed and Germany's situation became increasingly desperate, the ship's role shifted to evacuating German military personnel and civilians from areas threatened by advancing Allied forces. This was especially pertinent in the closing months of the war, as Soviet forces rapidly advanced into Eastern Europe, pushing into German-occupied territories and causing massive displacement of populations.

By early 1945, the Eastern Front was collapsing, and millions of German civilians, soldiers, and refugees were fleeing westward to escape the advancing Soviet troops. The German military initiated Operation Hannibal, one of the largest naval evacuation operations in history, aimed at rescuing as many people as possible from the encroaching Red Army. Ships of all kinds, including passenger liners, freighters, and fishing vessels, were pressed into service to transport the refugees and wounded soldiers across the Baltic Sea to safer territories in Germany and Denmark.

The MV Goya was among the ships mobilized for Operation Hannibal. On April 16, 1945, the ship departed from the port of Gotenhafen (now Gdynia, Poland) bound for the German port of Kiel. Onboard were thousands of refugees, mostly women, children, and elderly people, along with wounded soldiers and crew members. The exact number of passengers remains uncertain, but estimates suggest that the ship was carrying between 6,000 and 7,000 people, far exceeding its official capacity.

As the Goya made its way across the Baltic Sea, it was part of a larger convoy that included several other vessels, all attempting to navigate the dangerous waters under the constant threat of Soviet submarines. The Baltic Sea, particularly in the spring of 1945, was a perilous environment. Soviet submarines were actively patrolling the area, targeting German ships to disrupt the evacuation efforts and inflict maximum damage on the retreating forces.

At around 11:55 PM on April 16, 1945, the MV Goya was spotted by the Soviet submarine L-3, commanded by Captain Vladimir Konovalov. The L-3 was part of the Soviet Navy's Baltic Fleet, tasked with interdicting German evacuation routes. Upon identifying the Goya, Captain Konovalov ordered the submarine to launch a torpedo attack. The L-3 fired two torpedoes, both of which struck the Goya with devastating effect.

The first torpedo hit the ship in the forward section, causing a massive explosion that tore through the lower decks and cargo holds. The second torpedo struck near the engine room, further compromising the ship's structural integrity and causing catastrophic flooding. The Goya began to sink rapidly, taking on water at an alarming rate. Within minutes, the ship broke apart and sank beneath the icy waters of the Baltic Sea.

The chaos and panic that ensued were unimaginable. Thousands of people, many of whom were already traumatized by the horrors of war and displacement, found themselves struggling for survival in the frigid water. The lifeboats and life vests were woefully inadequate for the number of passengers onboard, and many people were trapped below decks as the ship went down. The cold waters of the Baltic Sea quickly claimed the lives of those who managed to escape the sinking vessel, and hypothermia set in rapidly.

Rescue efforts were limited and hampered by the ongoing naval conflict. Several nearby German ships attempted to save survivors but were constrained by the fear of further submarine attacks and the sheer scale of the disaster. Despite their efforts, only a small number of people were rescued. Estimates of the number of survivors vary, but it is generally believed that only around 183 people were saved from the Goya, while the vast majority—over 6,000 individuals—perished in the sinking.

The sinking of the MV Goya is considered one of the worst maritime disasters in history, not only in terms of the number of lives lost but also in the context of the suffering endured by those onboard. The tragedy underscores the immense human cost of war, particularly the final, desperate phase of World War II, as civilians and soldiers alike were caught in the crossfire of a collapsing front and a vengeful advance.

In the aftermath of the disaster, the sinking of the Goya remained relatively obscure compared to other wartime tragedies, partly due to the chaos and devastation of the closing months of the war. However, as time passed, efforts were made to document and remember the events of that fateful night. Survivor accounts and historical research have shed light on the tragedy, contributing to a fuller understanding of the disaster and its impact.

The MV Goya's sinking also had a broader significance in the context of maritime history. It highlighted the extreme dangers faced by civilian and military transport ships during wartime, particularly in contested waters. The loss of the Goya, along with other similar tragedies such as the sinking of the Wilhelm Gustloff earlier that year, emphasized the need for improved maritime safety protocols and the protection of non-combatant vessels during conflicts.

Memorials and commemorations have been established to honor the victims of the Goya disaster. In Germany and other parts of Europe, ceremonies are held to remember those who lost their lives in one of the darkest chapters of maritime history. These efforts ensure that the suffering and sacrifices of the passengers and crew are not forgotten, serving as a poignant reminder of the human cost of war.

The wreck of the MV Goya was discovered in the early 2000s, lying at a depth of approximately 76 meters (250 feet) in the Baltic Sea. The discovery of the wreck provided valuable information for historians and researchers, helping to piece together the events of the disaster and offering closure to some of the families of the victims. The site of the wreck has been designated as a war grave, and efforts have been made to protect it from disturbance, ensuring that it remains a solemn memorial to those who perished.

# Chapter 36: HMS Barham

HMS Barham, a Queen Elizabeth-class battleship of the Royal Navy, has a distinguished yet tragic history. Launched in 1914 during the early stages of World War I, Barham served in several key naval engagements before meeting a catastrophic end during World War II. The ship's sinking on November 25, 1941, by a German U-boat resulted in the loss of over 800 lives and became one of the most dramatic maritime disasters of the war. The detailed account of HMS Barham's service and its eventual sinking encapsulates the evolution of naval warfare, the perils of maritime conflict, and the heroism and sacrifice of those who served aboard her.

HMS Barham was constructed at John Brown & Company shipyard in Clydebank, Scotland. She was part of the Queen Elizabeth class, a group of five battleships intended to form the backbone of the Royal Navy's battle fleet. These ships were designed to be fast and heavily armed, embodying the principles of the "fast battleship" that combined speed with powerful armament and armor. Barham was laid down in February 1913, launched in December 1914, and commissioned in October 1915.

During World War I, Barham played a significant role in several naval engagements. She was part of the 5th Battle Squadron, attached to Admiral Sir David Beatty's Battlecruiser Fleet. Her most notable action during this period was at the Battle of Jutland in May 1916, the largest naval battle of the war. Barham, along with her sister ships, engaged the German High Seas Fleet in a series of intense exchanges of fire. Despite sustaining damage, Barham emerged from the battle relatively intact, showcasing the resilience and firepower of the Queen Elizabeth-class battleships.

Following World War I, Barham continued to serve with the Royal Navy during the interwar period. She underwent several refits to modernize her capabilities, including improvements to her armor, anti-aircraft armament, and fire control systems. These modifications were aimed at addressing the evolving threats and technological advancements in naval warfare. During the 1920s and 1930s, Barham was involved in various naval exercises and deployments, maintaining a presence in key strategic areas such as the Mediterranean.

With the outbreak of World War II in September 1939, HMS Barham was once again called into action. Initially, she was assigned to the Home Fleet, participating in the hunt for German surface raiders and protecting vital maritime routes. In December 1939, Barham was damaged by a torpedo from the German submarine U-30 but managed to return to port for repairs. After being repaired, she was reassigned to the Mediterranean Fleet, a critical theater of operations where the Royal Navy sought to maintain control of sea lanes and support Allied operations in North Africa and the Middle East.

In the Mediterranean, Barham participated in several significant naval engagements. One of the most notable was the Battle of Cape Matapan in March 1941, where the Royal Navy achieved a decisive victory over the Italian Navy. Barham played a key role in the battle, using her formidable firepower to help sink several Italian warships, including the heavy cruisers Zara, Fiume, and Pola. This victory helped to secure British naval dominance in the Mediterranean and disrupted Italian naval operations.

Despite these successes, the Mediterranean remained a highly contested and dangerous theater of war. The threat from Axis submarines and aircraft was ever-present, and the Royal Navy's operations were frequently hampered by these threats. On November 25, 1941, while operating off the coast of Egypt near Sidi Barrani, HMS Barham's fate was sealed. The ship was part of a fleet conducting patrols to counter Axis naval movements. Unbeknownst to the fleet, the German submarine U-331, commanded by Kapitänleutnant Hans-Diedrich von Tiesenhausen, had been tracking them.

U-331 managed to penetrate the escort screen surrounding Barham and launched a salvo of four torpedoes. Three of these torpedoes found their mark, striking Barham on her port side. The explosions caused massive damage, and the ship began to list heavily to port. Within minutes, the situation aboard Barham became dire as fires broke out and the order was given to abandon ship. Tragically, the severity of the damage meant that there was little time for an orderly evacuation.

As Barham continued to list, a catastrophic explosion occurred in her magazine, the compartment where ammunition was stored. This explosion was so powerful that it ripped the ship apart, and Barham capsized and sank rapidly. The destruction was filmed by a newsreel cameraman aboard one of the escorting ships, and the dramatic footage later became one of the most widely recognized and harrowing visual records of a battleship's sinking during the war.

The sinking of HMS Barham resulted in the loss of 841 men, including the ship's captain, Captain Geoffrey Cooke, and a significant portion of her crew. The sudden and violent nature of the sinking meant that many of the crew were unable to escape the ship. The Royal Navy conducted rescue operations, but the chaos and rapid sinking limited the number of survivors. The loss of Barham was a severe blow to the Royal Navy and a stark reminder of the deadly effectiveness of submarine warfare.

In the immediate aftermath, the Admiralty imposed a news blackout on the sinking of Barham. This decision was made to prevent the information from demoralizing the British public and to ensure that the news did not reach the enemy, potentially encouraging further submarine attacks. The families of those lost were notified privately, and the sinking was not publicly acknowledged until late January 1942, when the Admiralty issued a statement.

The sinking of HMS Barham had several significant implications. It underscored the vulnerability of even the most powerful warships to submarine attacks, a lesson that would influence naval strategy and ship design in the years to come. The loss also highlighted the critical importance of effective anti-submarine measures, leading to increased efforts to develop and deploy more advanced sonar, depth charges, and other anti-submarine technologies.

The bravery and sacrifice of Barham's crew have been commemorated in various ways over the years. Memorial services and ceremonies have been held to honor those who lost their lives, and their names are inscribed on naval memorials, including the Portsmouth Naval Memorial and the Chatham Naval Memorial. The dramatic footage of Barham's sinking has been used in documentaries and educational materials to illustrate the dangers faced by naval forces during World War II and to pay tribute to the sailors who served and sacrificed.

In addition to its immediate impact, the story of HMS Barham has become part of the broader narrative of World War II and the history of naval warfare. The ship's service history, from its participation in the Battle of Jutland to its final engagements in the Mediterranean, reflects the evolution of naval strategy and technology during the first half of the 20th century. The sinking of Barham also serves as a poignant reminder of the human cost of war and the courage of those who serve at sea.

In historical context, the loss of HMS Barham fits into a pattern of significant naval losses during World War II, including other battleships, aircraft carriers, and cruisers that fell victim to submarine attacks, air strikes, and surface engagements. These losses, while tragic, spurred innovations in naval tactics and technology, ultimately contributing to the development of more resilient and capable naval forces.

The legacy of HMS Barham endures in the annals of naval history. The ship's service, from World War I through World War II, represents a period of intense and rapid change in maritime warfare. The lessons learned from her engagements and ultimate loss continue to inform naval strategy and the design of warships. The memory of Barham and her crew is preserved through memorials, historical research, and the ongoing efforts of naval historians and enthusiasts to document and share the stories of those who served aboard her.

# Chapter 37: SS Cap Arcona

The story of the SS Cap Arcona is one of the most tragic and horrific maritime disasters of World War II, highlighting the grim reality of the war's final days and the severe cost of human lives. The Cap Arcona, a German luxury ocean liner, was transformed into a floating concentration camp, and its sinking on May 3, 1945, resulted in the death of thousands of concentration camp prisoners, making it one of the deadliest maritime disasters ever recorded. This tragedy is a stark reminder of the atrocities committed during the Holocaust and the chaos that engulfed Europe as the war drew to a close.

The SS Cap Arcona was built in 1927 by the Blohm & Voss shipyard in Hamburg, Germany, for the Hamburg-South America Line. It was one of the most elegant and luxurious liners of its time, designed to operate on the South Atlantic route between Germany and South America. The ship was 206 meters (676 feet) long, with a beam of 25 meters (82 feet), and had a gross tonnage of 27,561 tons. The Cap Arcona could accommodate 1,315 passengers and had a crew of 450. It was celebrated for its luxurious amenities, including lavish dining rooms, swimming pools, and spacious cabins, earning it the nickname "Queen of the South Atlantic."

The Cap Arcona enjoyed several years of success as a passenger liner, carrying wealthy passengers on transatlantic voyages and contributing to Germany's maritime prestige. However, with the outbreak of World War II in 1939, the ship's role changed dramatically. The German Navy requisitioned the Cap Arcona for use as an accommodation ship and, later, as a troop transport vessel. Throughout the war, the ship was involved in various naval operations, including the transport of soldiers and supplies.

As the war neared its end and Germany faced imminent defeat, the Nazi regime's desperation became increasingly apparent. The Allied forces were advancing on all fronts, and the Soviet Army was closing in on Germany from the east. In a final, macabre act of brutality, the Nazis began evacuating concentration camps in Poland and moving prisoners westward, away from the advancing Soviet forces. These evacuations, often referred to as death marches, resulted in the deaths of tens of thousands of prisoners due to exhaustion, starvation, and summary executions.

In April 1945, as part of this chaotic evacuation effort, the SS Cap Arcona, along with other ships, was repurposed to hold concentration camp prisoners. The ship was anchored in the Bay of Lübeck on the Baltic Sea, near Neustadt, along with several other vessels, including the Thielbek and Athen, all of which were used to accommodate thousands of prisoners from various concentration camps, including Neuengamme and Stutthof.

The conditions aboard the Cap Arcona were appalling. The ship, designed for luxury travel, was now overcrowded with emaciated and weakened prisoners who had endured the unimaginable horrors of the concentration camps. There was a severe lack of food, water, and medical supplies, and many of the prisoners were suffering from diseases such as typhus. The guards, consisting of SS personnel and members of the Hitler Youth, showed no mercy and continued to brutalize the prisoners. The Cap Arcona had become a floating hell, a stark contrast to its former grandeur.

On May 3, 1945, the British Royal Air Force (RAF) launched an operation targeting German shipping in the Baltic Sea. The objective was to prevent the escape of high-ranking Nazis and to stop any potential reinforcement or evacuation efforts by sea. Unfortunately, the RAF had not been informed about the presence of concentration camp prisoners aboard the Cap Arcona and the other ships anchored in the Bay of Lübeck. Consequently, the ships were mistaken for legitimate military targets.

At around 2:30 PM, a squadron of RAF Typhoon fighter-bombers from No. 83 Group, led by Group Captain Johnny Baldwin, began their attack on the ships. The Cap Arcona, along with the Thielbek and Athen, was strafed and bombed with rockets and machine-gun fire. The Cap Arcona was hit multiple times, resulting in massive fires and explosions that quickly spread throughout the ship. The chaos and destruction were overwhelming, and the prisoners, already weakened and terrified, were trapped in a burning, sinking vessel.

As the Cap Arcona was engulfed in flames, prisoners who managed to escape the inferno were faced with the freezing waters of the Baltic Sea. Many were unable to swim due to their weakened state, and those who did reach the water were often shot at by the guards or strafed by the attacking aircraft. The scenes of horror and despair were unimaginable, with prisoners struggling to survive amidst the flames and gunfire.

The attack on the Cap Arcona, Thielbek, and Athen resulted in the deaths of an estimated 7,000 to 8,000 concentration camp prisoners. The majority of the prisoners aboard the Cap Arcona perished either in the inferno or in the icy waters. Only a few hundred survivors were rescued by German ships and local fishermen who braved the dangers to save as many lives as possible. The Thielbek also suffered a significant loss of life, with approximately 2,800 prisoners perishing in the attack. The Athen, while heavily damaged, did not suffer as catastrophic a loss of life as the other two vessels.

The sinking of the Cap Arcona is one of the deadliest maritime disasters in history, not only in terms of the sheer number of lives lost but also because of the harrowing circumstances under which the disaster occurred. The tragedy was compounded by the fact that the prisoners, who had already endured unimaginable suffering in the concentration camps, met their end in such a brutal and senseless manner, just days before the end of the war in Europe.

In the aftermath of the disaster, the full extent of the tragedy slowly emerged. The surviving prisoners, many of whom were severely injured and traumatized, were taken to hospitals and makeshift shelters. The bodies of the victims washed ashore for weeks, creating a grim and haunting reminder of the atrocity. Local residents, Allied soldiers, and humanitarian workers were left to deal with the aftermath, recovering bodies and providing aid to the survivors.

The British authorities, upon realizing the enormity of the tragedy, conducted investigations to understand what had transpired. It became clear that the lack of communication and the fog of war had contributed to the mistaken attack on the Cap Arcona and the other ships. The RAF pilots involved in the attack were not informed about the presence of concentration camp prisoners, and the information about the ships' true purpose had not reached the appropriate channels.

The sinking of the Cap Arcona was initially overshadowed by the broader context of the war's end and the liberation of the concentration camps. However, over time, the story gained recognition as one of the many atrocities of the Holocaust and the final days of World War II. Memorials and commemorations have been established to honor the memory of the victims. In Neustadt, where many of the bodies washed ashore, a memorial stands to remember those who perished in the tragedy. The Cap Arcona's wreck itself lies at the bottom of the Bay of Lübeck, a silent witness to the horror that unfolded.

The legacy of the Cap Arcona disaster is a poignant reminder of the brutality and senselessness of war. It underscores the importance of preserving historical memory and ensuring that such tragedies are not forgotten. The story of the Cap Arcona is also a testament to the resilience and courage of the survivors, who, despite enduring unimaginable suffering, managed to live through one of the darkest chapters in human history.

In historical context, the sinking of the Cap Arcona fits into the broader narrative of World War II's final days, marked by chaos, desperation, and a profound disregard for human life by the Nazi regime. It is a stark illustration of the atrocities committed during the Holocaust and the indiscriminate nature of war's violence. The tragedy serves as a somber reminder of the need for vigilance against hatred, intolerance, and the dehumanization of individuals based on race, religion, or political beliefs.

# Chapter 38: SS Norway

The SS Norway, originally launched as the SS France in 1960, is a vessel that exemplifies the grandeur and evolution of ocean liners throughout the latter half of the 20th century and into the early 21st century. Renowned for its elegance, size, and luxurious amenities, the ship experienced a remarkable transformation from a transatlantic liner to a cruise ship before meeting its unfortunate demise in 2003. The story of the SS Norway encapsulates the changing nature of maritime travel, the rise and fall of ocean liners, and the challenges faced by the cruise industry.

The SS France was built by the Chantiers de l'Atlantique shipyard in Saint-Nazaire, France, and was launched on May 11, 1960. At the time of its launch, the France was one of the longest and most luxurious passenger ships in the world. Measuring 315.66 meters (1,037 feet) in length, with a beam of 33.7 meters (110 feet), and a gross tonnage of 66,343 tons, the SS France was a symbol of national pride and technological prowess for France. The ship was designed to operate on the transatlantic route between Le Havre and New York City, offering passengers a combination of speed, comfort, and opulence.

The interior of the SS France was a marvel of mid-20th-century design, featuring lavish dining rooms, elegant lounges, and spacious cabins. The ship could accommodate up to 2,044 passengers and had a crew of 1,100. The public spaces were adorned with art and décor that reflected the ship's French heritage, including works by prominent artists and designers. The France quickly became a favorite among transatlantic travelers, known for its impeccable service and luxurious amenities.

However, the advent of jet travel in the 1960s and 1970s led to a decline in demand for transatlantic ocean liner services. Airlines offered faster and more convenient travel options, and many iconic liners struggled to remain profitable. The SS France was no exception.

Despite its popularity and grandeur, the ship faced financial difficulties as passenger numbers dwindled. In 1974, after just 14 years of service, the SS France was withdrawn from transatlantic service and laid up in the port of Le Havre.

For five years, the SS France remained in limbo, its future uncertain. The ship's fate took a positive turn in 1979 when it was purchased by Norwegian Caribbean Line (NCL), a company that would later become Norwegian Cruise Line. NCL saw potential in the grand ocean liner and embarked on an ambitious project to convert it into a cruise ship. The ship was renamed SS Norway and underwent extensive renovations to transform it from a transatlantic liner to a modern cruise vessel.

The conversion of the SS France into the SS Norway involved significant modifications. The ship's passenger capacity was increased to over 2,200, and its public spaces were updated to meet the needs and expectations of cruise passengers. New amenities were added, including multiple swimming pools, casinos, theaters, and a variety of dining options. Despite these changes, the SS Norway retained much of its original elegance and charm, with many of its original art and design elements preserved.

In 1980, the SS Norway entered service as a cruise ship, operating primarily in the Caribbean. The ship's size and grandeur made it a popular choice among cruisers, and it quickly became one of the flagship vessels of the NCL fleet. The Norway offered a unique blend of traditional ocean liner elegance and modern cruise ship amenities, attracting a diverse range of passengers. Its itineraries included popular Caribbean destinations, as well as occasional transatlantic crossings and world cruises.

Throughout the 1980s and 1990s, the SS Norway continued to be a beloved and successful cruise ship. It played a significant role in the growth and development of the modern cruise industry, setting new standards for luxury and service. The ship's distinctive silhouette and storied history made it an icon of maritime travel, and it garnered a loyal following of passengers who appreciated its blend of classic and contemporary experiences.

However, as the cruise industry evolved and newer, more advanced ships entered service, the SS Norway faced increasing challenges. By the late 1990s, the ship was showing signs of age, and maintaining its aging infrastructure became increasingly costly. Despite efforts to modernize and upgrade the vessel, the Norway struggled to compete with newer, purpose-built cruise ships that offered more amenities and greater efficiency.

In May 2003, the SS Norway was docked in the Port of Miami when disaster struck. A catastrophic boiler explosion occurred in the ship's engine room, resulting in the deaths of eight crew members and injuries to several others. The explosion caused significant damage to the ship's propulsion system and other critical infrastructure, rendering it inoperable. The incident marked the end of the SS Norway's operational career and set off a series of events that would ultimately lead to the ship's demise.

Following the explosion, NCL faced difficult decisions regarding the future of the SS Norway. The extent of the damage and the cost of repairs made it economically unfeasible to restore the ship to service. In September 2003, the decision was made to retire the SS Norway permanently. The ship was towed to Bremerhaven, Germany, where it remained laid up while various plans for its future were considered, including potential conversion into a hotel ship or museum.

Despite efforts to find a viable future for the SS Norway, none of the proposed plans came to fruition. In 2006, the ship was sold to a scrap merchant and subsequently towed to Alang, India, one of the world's largest ship-breaking yards. The news of the SS Norway's impending scrapping was met with sadness and nostalgia by maritime enthusiasts and former passengers who had fond memories of the iconic vessel. Efforts to save the ship through preservation campaigns were ultimately unsuccessful.

In August 2006, the SS Norway arrived in Alang, where it was dismantled and scrapped. The process of breaking up the ship took several months, during which time valuable materials and components were salvaged. The scrapping of the SS Norway marked the end of an era, as one of the last great ocean liners was reduced to pieces. The ship's legacy, however, lives on in the memories of those who sailed on her and in the history of maritime travel.

The story of the SS Norway is a reflection of the broader changes and challenges faced by the maritime industry over the course of the 20th century. The ship's transformation from the SS France, a symbol of national pride and technological achievement, to the SS Norway, a beloved cruise ship, highlights the adaptability and resilience of ocean liners. It also underscores the impact of technological advancements and changing travel preferences on the maritime industry.

The SS Norway's journey from a luxurious transatlantic liner to a popular cruise ship and ultimately to a dismantled relic is a poignant reminder of the impermanence of even the grandest achievements. The ship's legacy endures through the memories of those who experienced its elegance and grandeur, as well as through the historical records and artifacts that preserve its story.

# Chapter 39: MS Herald of Free Enterprise

The MS Herald of Free Enterprise disaster, which occurred on March 6, 1987, is one of the most significant and tragic maritime incidents in modern history. The ship, a roll-on/roll-off (Ro-Ro) ferry operated by Townsend Thoresen, capsized shortly after leaving the Belgian port of Zeebrugge, resulting in the deaths of 193 passengers and crew. This catastrophic event led to a profound reevaluation of safety regulations in the ferry industry and highlighted the human and systemic failures that contributed to the disaster. The detailed account of the MS Herald of Free Enterprise encompasses the ship's history, the sequence of events leading up to the disaster, the immediate aftermath, and the far-reaching implications for maritime safety.

The MS Herald of Free Enterprise was built in 1980 by Schichau-Unterweser in Bremerhaven, West Germany. It was one of three sister ships, along with the Pride of Free Enterprise and Spirit of Free Enterprise, designed for Townsend Thoresen to operate on the cross-Channel route between Dover, England, and Calais, France. The ship was 131 meters (430 feet) long, with a beam of 23 meters (75 feet), and a gross tonnage of 7,951 tons. As a Ro-Ro ferry, it was designed to transport both passengers and vehicles, with large doors at the bow and stern to allow for quick loading and unloading.

The Herald of Free Enterprise had a capacity of 1,400 passengers and could carry 340 cars or a combination of cars and trucks. The ship was equipped with several decks, including vehicle decks and passenger accommodation areas, which featured lounges, restaurants, and other amenities. The ferry was designed to provide efficient and convenient transportation across the English Channel, a vital link for passengers and goods between the UK and continental Europe.

The disaster unfolded on the evening of March 6, 1987. The Herald of Free Enterprise had completed the loading process at Zeebrugge and was scheduled to depart for Dover. The ferry was carrying 459 passengers, 80 crew members, and 81 vehicles. As the ship prepared to leave port, a series of critical errors and oversights set the stage for the impending tragedy. One of the most crucial lapses was the failure to close the bow doors, which were left open due to a breakdown in communication and procedural shortcomings.

At approximately 6:05 PM, the Herald of Free Enterprise left its berth and began moving through the harbor. Unbeknownst to the crew on the bridge, the bow doors remained open, allowing water to enter the vehicle deck. This design flaw, where the vehicle deck spanned the full width of the ship, created a vulnerability: any significant ingress of water could quickly destabilize the vessel. The ferry accelerated to its cruising speed, causing more water to flood the vehicle deck. Within minutes, the ship began to list to port, and the situation rapidly deteriorated.

At 6:28 PM, just 90 seconds after clearing the harbor, the Herald of Free Enterprise capsized and came to rest on its side in shallow water approximately half a mile from the shore. The suddenness of the capsize meant that many passengers and crew were trapped inside the ship with little time to react. The cold waters of the North Sea, coupled with the rapid flooding of the ferry's interior, created a deadly environment. Survivors described scenes of chaos and desperation as people struggled to escape the tilting and flooding compartments.

Rescue operations began almost immediately, with local vessels, helicopters, and emergency services responding to the distress call. Despite the swift response, the challenging conditions and the speed at which the ship capsized hampered rescue efforts. Many passengers were unable to escape the ship, and the freezing water temperatures led to hypothermia and drowning. The final death toll reached 193, making it one of the worst maritime disasters in British peacetime history.

In the aftermath of the disaster, a public inquiry was launched to investigate the causes and identify those responsible. The inquiry, chaired by Lord Justice Sheen, revealed a series of systemic failures and human errors that contributed to the tragedy. The most glaring oversight was the failure to close the bow doors before departure. It was determined that Assistant Boatswain Mark Stanley, who was responsible for closing the doors, had fallen asleep in his cabin. Furthermore, there was no system in place to ensure that the bow doors were closed before the ship left port, a critical lapse in operational procedures.

The inquiry also highlighted issues with the design of the ship and the broader culture within Townsend Thoresen. The company was criticized for prioritizing speed and efficiency over safety, with practices that encouraged quick turnarounds and insufficient attention to safety protocols. The management's focus on maintaining tight schedules led to inadequate training and communication among the crew, contributing to the oversight that resulted in the disaster.

The findings of the Sheen Inquiry led to significant legal and regulatory repercussions. Townsend Thoresen faced intense scrutiny and criticism, and the company underwent a rebranding, eventually becoming P&O European Ferries. Several individuals were prosecuted for negligence, although no criminal convictions were ultimately secured. The disaster also prompted a thorough review of safety regulations for Ro-Ro ferries.

One of the most important outcomes was the introduction of new international safety standards under the auspices of the International Maritime Organization (IMO). The SOLAS (Safety of Life at Sea) Convention was amended to include stricter requirements for the design and operation of Ro-Ro ferries. These amendments mandated improved watertight integrity, better evacuation procedures, and enhanced stability standards to prevent similar incidents in the future. Additionally, the International Safety Management (ISM) Code was developed to promote a culture of safety within shipping companies, emphasizing the importance of safety management systems and regular audits.

The disaster also had a profound impact on the public perception of ferry safety. For passengers, the realization that such a catastrophic event could occur so quickly and with such devastating consequences was a sobering reminder of the inherent risks of maritime travel. This shift in awareness led to greater demand for transparency and accountability from ferry operators, as well as increased vigilance from regulatory bodies.

Over the years, the legacy of the Herald of Free Enterprise disaster has been commemorated in various ways. Memorials have been established to honor the victims, and the incident has been studied extensively in maritime safety courses and disaster management programs. The lessons learned from the tragedy continue to inform the design and operation of Ro-Ro ferries, ensuring that safety remains a paramount concern.

In historical context, the Herald of Free Enterprise disaster is a stark illustration of the interplay between human error, systemic failures, and design flaws in maritime operations. It underscores the critical importance of adhering to safety protocols and maintaining robust systems to prevent lapses that can lead to catastrophic outcomes. The incident also highlights the role of regulatory bodies in enforcing safety standards and the need for continuous improvement in maritime safety practices.

The story of the MS Herald of Free Enterprise serves as a poignant reminder of the fragility of human life and the devastating impact of preventable accidents. The loss of 193 lives is a tragic testament to the consequences of negligence and the vital importance of vigilance and accountability in all aspects of maritime operations. As the maritime industry continues to evolve, the lessons from the Herald of Free

Enterprise disaster remain relevant, guiding efforts to enhance safety and protect the lives of passengers and crew.

161

# Chapter 40: USS Thresher

The USS Thresher (SSN-593) was a nuclear-powered attack submarine of the United States Navy that tragically sank during deep-diving tests on April 10, 1963, leading to the loss of all 129 crew members and civilian technicians aboard. This disaster remains one of the deadliest submarine incidents in history and prompted significant changes in submarine design, maintenance, and safety protocols. The story of the USS Thresher encompasses its construction, operational history, the events leading to its sinking, the investigation and findings, and the far-reaching implications for submarine safety and naval procedures.

The USS Thresher was the lead vessel of its class, representing a new generation of submarines designed to be faster, quieter, and more capable than its predecessors. Built by the Portsmouth Naval Shipyard in Kittery, Maine, the Thresher was launched on July 9, 1960, and commissioned on August 3, 1961. The submarine measured 278 feet (85 meters) in length, had a beam of 31 feet (9.4 meters), and displaced approximately 3,500 tons when submerged. Powered by a S5W reactor, the Thresher was capable of reaching speeds over 20 knots while submerged and could dive to depths greater than previous classes of submarines.

The Thresher was designed with several advanced features intended to enhance its stealth and combat capabilities. These included a quieter propulsion system, improved sonar, and advanced weapon systems, including torpedoes and anti-ship missiles. The submarine's hull was constructed using high-strength HY-80 steel, which allowed it to operate at greater depths. The Thresher was intended to counter the growing threat of Soviet submarines during the Cold War, providing the U.S. Navy with a potent tool for undersea warfare.

After its commissioning, the USS Thresher underwent a series of trials and shakedown cruises to test its systems and performance. These included deep-diving tests to ensure the submarine could safely operate at its designed depths. Initial trials revealed several issues that required correction, including problems with the reactor plant and the submarine's control systems. Despite these challenges, the Thresher was considered a state-of-the-art vessel and a significant step forward in submarine technology.

On April 9, 1963, the USS Thresher departed from Portsmouth Naval Shipyard to conduct deep-diving tests off the coast of Cape Cod, Massachusetts. Accompanying the Thresher was the submarine rescue ship USS Skylark (ASR-20), which was tasked with supporting the submarine during its test dives. The following day, April 10, the Thresher began its descent to its test depth, monitored by the Skylark.

At approximately 7:47 AM, the Thresher reported reaching a depth of 1,000 feet (300 meters) and began a series of system checks. Communication between the Thresher and the Skylark was maintained via underwater telephone, allowing the submarine to report its status and any issues encountered. At 9:13 AM, the Thresher transmitted a garbled message indicating a minor problem: "Experiencing minor difficulties, have positive up angle, attempting to blow." This message suggested that the submarine was attempting to surface by using its ballast tanks to expel water and increase buoyancy.

Shortly thereafter, communication with the Thresher was lost. The Skylark attempted to reestablish contact, but all efforts were unsuccessful. At 11:04 AM, the Skylark reported to naval authorities that the Thresher was presumed lost. A massive search and rescue operation was launched, involving numerous ships, aircraft, and submarines, but no survivors were found. The wreckage of the Thresher was eventually located on the seafloor at a depth of approximately 8,400 feet (2,560 meters).

The loss of the USS Thresher prompted a thorough investigation to determine the cause of the disaster. The inquiry, led by Admiral Hyman G. Rickover, often referred to as the father of the nuclear Navy, and the Thresher Court of Inquiry, identified several factors that contributed to the sinking. The investigation revealed that a failure in a silver-brazed joint in the submarine's engine room piping system had likely caused a high-pressure seawater leak. This leak led to a loss of power and control, preventing the submarine from surfacing.

The inquiry found that the Thresher's crew had attempted to blow the ballast tanks using the high-pressure air system, but ice formation caused by the rapid expansion of air had clogged the system, rendering it ineffective. The loss of power also disabled the submarine's propulsion, leaving it unable to maintain depth control. As the Thresher descended uncontrollably, the increasing pressure caused further structural failures, ultimately leading to the implosion of the submarine.

The findings of the Thresher disaster had profound implications for submarine safety and design. The investigation highlighted several deficiencies in the construction and testing of submarines, including inadequate quality control in the fabrication of components and insufficient testing of critical systems under realistic conditions. The disaster also underscored the need for improved emergency procedures and crew training to handle catastrophic failures.

In response to the Thresher disaster, the U.S. Navy launched the SUBSAFE program, a comprehensive safety initiative aimed at preventing similar incidents in the future. The SUBSAFE program established rigorous standards for the design, construction, and maintenance of submarines, with a focus on ensuring the integrity of the pressure hull and critical systems. Key elements of the program included enhanced quality control measures, stringent testing protocols, and the use of high-reliability components.

The SUBSAFE program also mandated regular inspections and certification of submarines, ensuring that any potential issues were identified and addressed before they could lead to catastrophic failures. The program's emphasis on safety and reliability has been credited with significantly improving the safety record of the U.S. submarine fleet.

Since the implementation of SUBSAFE, there has not been another peacetime loss of a U.S. Navy submarine.

The legacy of the USS Thresher extends beyond its impact on submarine safety. The disaster had a profound effect on the families of the 129 men who perished, and memorials have been established to honor their memory. The USS Thresher Memorial at Arlington National Cemetery, dedicated in 1964, serves as a somber reminder of the lives lost and the sacrifices made by those who serve in the silent service.

The Thresher disaster also underscored the importance of transparency and accountability in military operations. The U.S. Navy's willingness to thoroughly investigate the incident and implement sweeping changes demonstrated a commitment to learning from the tragedy and preventing future losses. This approach has been emulated by other navies and organizations worldwide, contributing to broader improvements in safety and operational standards.

In historical context, the USS Thresher disaster is a stark reminder of the inherent risks of submarine operations and the need for continual vigilance in maintaining the highest standards of safety and reliability. The lessons learned from the Thresher have been instrumental in shaping the modern submarine fleet, ensuring that subsequent generations of submariners are better protected against the dangers of undersea warfare.

The story of the USS Thresher is also a testament to the resilience and determination of the U.S. Navy and its personnel. Despite the tragedy, the Navy's commitment to advancing submarine technology and maintaining a formidable undersea force remained unwavering. The advancements made in the wake of the Thresher disaster have contributed to the development of some of the most advanced and capable submarines in the world, ensuring the continued dominance of the U.S. Navy in undersea warfare.

# Chapter 41: SS Great Eastern

The SS Great Eastern, originally named Leviathan, stands as one of the most ambitious and groundbreaking ships of the 19th century, embodying the visionary spirit and engineering prowess of its era. Conceived by the renowned British engineer Isambard Kingdom Brunel, the Great Eastern was a marvel of maritime engineering, notable for its enormous size, innovative design, and the audacity of its purpose. The story of the SS Great Eastern encompasses its conception, construction, operational history, significant achievements, and the challenges it faced throughout its existence, making it a fascinating chapter in the history of maritime technology.

Isambard Kingdom Brunel, one of the foremost engineers of the 19th century, conceived the idea for the SS Great Eastern in the early 1850s. At the time, Brunel had already established a reputation for his work on railways, bridges, and the Great Western Railway. His previous ventures into maritime engineering included the design and construction of the SS Great Western and the SS Great Britain, both of which were pioneering ships in their own right. However, Brunel's vision for the Great Eastern was far more ambitious: he envisioned a ship capable of carrying passengers and cargo between England and Australia without the need for refueling, a feat that would require a vessel of unprecedented size and capacity.

The design of the Great Eastern was revolutionary in several respects. At a time when most ships were built using wood, Brunel opted for an iron hull, which offered greater strength and durability. The ship was also designed with a double hull, an innovative feature that provided extra protection against damage and leaks. This double hull consisted of an inner and outer layer of iron plates, with a space in between that could be used for ballast or to improve buoyancy. The Great Eastern was also equipped with both paddle wheels and a screw propeller, allowing it to be powered by either method or both simultaneously. This dual propulsion system was intended to provide greater speed and maneuverability, as well as a measure of redundancy in case one system failed.

Construction of the Great Eastern began in May 1854 at the Millwall Iron Works on the River Thames in London. The ship was designed to be 692 feet (211 meters) long, with a beam of 83 feet (25 meters) and a height of 58 feet (18 meters) from keel to deck. It had a gross tonnage of 18,915 tons, making it by far the largest ship in the world at the time. The sheer size of the vessel presented numerous engineering and logistical challenges. For instance, the shipyard had to be specially modified to accommodate the construction of such a large ship, including the installation of massive cranes and other heavy machinery.

The launch of the Great Eastern was a monumental event, but it did not go smoothly. Originally scheduled for November 3, 1857, the launch was delayed due to technical difficulties and problems with the launching gear. The massive ship had to be launched sideways into the Thames, a method that was fraught with risks. After several failed attempts and much controversy, the Great Eastern finally entered the water on January 31, 1858, but the delays and additional costs had already taken a toll on Brunel and his financial backers.

Once launched, the Great Eastern faced further challenges during its fitting out and sea trials. The ship was equipped with five funnels, two paddle wheels, and a four-bladed screw propeller, along with six masts that could carry a full complement of sails. Despite these impressive features, the Great Eastern was plagued by technical problems, including issues with its engines and steering mechanisms. During its maiden voyage in September 1859, the ship experienced a boiler explosion that killed several crew members and caused significant damage. This incident, coupled with ongoing financial difficulties, cast a shadow over the ship's early years.

Despite these setbacks, the Great Eastern was put into service as a passenger and cargo liner, making its first transatlantic crossing in June 1860. The ship's size and capacity allowed it to carry up to 4,000 passengers and vast quantities of cargo, making it ideal for long-distance voyages. However, the Great Eastern's commercial success was limited by a number of factors, including competition from other shipping lines, high operating costs, and its own reputation for technical problems. The ship was often underutilized, and its owners struggled to make it profitable.

The turning point for the Great Eastern came in the mid-1860s when it was repurposed for a new and crucial role: laying submarine telegraph cables. The ship's immense size and stability made it ideally suited for this task, which required the ability to carry and deploy long lengths of heavy cable across vast distances. In 1865, the Great Eastern was chartered by the Atlantic Telegraph Company to lay a transatlantic telegraph cable between Ireland and Newfoundland. This project was of immense strategic and commercial importance, as it aimed to establish direct communication between Europe and North America.

The first attempt to lay the cable in 1865 ended in failure when the cable snapped and was lost. However, undeterred by this setback, the Atlantic Telegraph Company undertook a second attempt in 1866. This time, the Great Eastern successfully laid the cable, completing the first reliable transatlantic telegraph connection. The success of this mission was a major milestone in global communications, significantly reducing the time required to send messages between Europe and North America. The Great Eastern's role in this achievement cemented its place in maritime history as a pioneering vessel.

Following the successful laying of the transatlantic cable, the Great Eastern continued to be used for similar projects, including the laying of cables in the Mediterranean and the Indian Ocean. Despite its success in these endeavors, the ship's commercial viability as a passenger liner remained limited. The Great Eastern changed hands several times and was eventually used as a floating billboard and exhibition ship.

By the late 1870s, the Great Eastern had become obsolete, superseded by newer and more efficient ships. In 1888, the ship was sold for scrap and dismantled at a shipbreaking yard in Liverpool. The dismantling process took nearly two years, a testament to the ship's immense size and robust construction.

The legacy of the SS Great Eastern extends far beyond its operational history. The ship's innovative design and engineering advancements influenced the development of future ocean liners and laid the groundwork for the modern shipping industry. The use of iron hulls, double hulls, and combined propulsion systems became standard features in later ships, reflecting the pioneering spirit of the Great Eastern.

Moreover, the Great Eastern's role in laying transatlantic telegraph cables marked a turning point in global communications. The successful establishment of a reliable telegraph connection between Europe and North America revolutionized international communication, paving the way for the interconnected world we live in today. The ship's contribution to this achievement is a testament to the vision and ingenuity of Isambard Kingdom Brunel and the engineers and workers who brought his ambitious project to life.

In historical context, the SS Great Eastern represents both the triumphs and challenges of technological innovation in the 19th century. The ship's construction and operational history reflect the broader trends of industrialization, globalization, and the quest for progress that characterized the Victorian era. The Great Eastern's story is also a reminder of the risks and uncertainties inherent in pushing the boundaries of what is possible, as well as the resilience and determination required to overcome obstacles and achieve great feats.

# Chapter 42: USS Cole

The USS Cole (DDG-67) is an Arleigh Burke-class guided-missile destroyer of the United States Navy, best known for the terrorist attack it endured on October 12, 2000, while refueling in the port of Aden, Yemen. This tragic event resulted in the deaths of 17 sailors and injuries to 39 others, marking one of the most significant terrorist attacks against the U.S. Navy in modern history. The incident not only highlighted vulnerabilities in military operations but also had profound implications for U.S. naval policies, counterterrorism strategies, and geopolitical relations. The story of the USS Cole encompasses its construction and commissioning, operational history, the details of the attack, the immediate and long-term responses, and its enduring legacy.

The USS Cole was ordered as part of the U.S. Navy's efforts to modernize its fleet with highly capable and versatile warships. Named after Marine Sergeant Darrell S. Cole, a Medal of Honor recipient killed in action during World War II, the ship was laid down on February 28, 1994, at the Ingalls Shipbuilding yard in Pascagoula, Mississippi. The Cole was launched on February 10, 1995, and commissioned on June 8, 1996. As an Arleigh Burke-class destroyer, the Cole was equipped with advanced Aegis combat systems, sophisticated radar and sonar equipment, and a variety of armaments, including Tomahawk cruise missiles, anti-aircraft missiles, and anti-submarine torpedoes. These capabilities made it a formidable vessel designed for a wide range of missions, from peacetime presence to power projection and warfighting.

In its early years, the USS Cole participated in various exercises and operations, contributing to the U.S. Navy's global presence and readiness. The ship was involved in training exercises with allied navies, anti-piracy missions, and enforcement of United Nations sanctions. These activities underscored the destroyer's role in maintaining maritime security and projecting American naval power around the world.

The fateful events leading to the attack on the USS Cole began with its deployment to the Arabian Sea as part of the U.S. Navy's ongoing operations in the region. On October 12, 2000, the Cole was en route to the Persian Gulf to support the enforcement of U.N. sanctions against Iraq. As part of its routine operations, the ship made a scheduled stop in the port of Aden, Yemen, for refueling. The port was considered a relatively safe location, and the Cole had visited it previously without incident. However, this perception of safety would soon be shattered.

At around 11:18 AM local time, while the Cole was moored to a refueling buoy in Aden harbor, a small boat approached the ship's port side. The boat, manned by two suicide bombers, carried explosives estimated to weigh between 400 and 700 pounds. The attackers brought the boat alongside the destroyer and detonated the explosives, resulting in a massive explosion that tore a 40-by-60-foot hole in the ship's hull, near the waterline. The blast caused significant damage to the Cole, flooding the engine room and nearby compartments, and leading to the deaths of 17 sailors. Another 39 crew members were injured, some critically.

The immediate aftermath of the explosion was chaotic and dire. The blast had caused the ship to list, and there was a risk of further flooding and potential sinking. The crew, however, responded with remarkable bravery and professionalism. Damage control teams quickly mobilized to stabilize the ship, control flooding, and assist the wounded. Their swift actions were crucial in preventing the ship from sinking and saving the lives of many injured personnel. The crew's efforts were supported by nearby vessels and port authorities, who provided additional assistance and medical care.

The attack on the USS Cole sent shockwaves through the U.S. military and government. It was quickly determined that the attack was an act of terrorism, and suspicion fell on the terrorist organization al-Qaeda, which had been responsible for previous attacks on U.S. interests, including the 1998 bombings of the U.S. embassies in Kenya and Tanzania. Investigations by the Federal Bureau of Investigation (FBI) and other agencies confirmed that the attack was orchestrated by al-Qaeda operatives, and several individuals involved in the planning and execution of the attack were later identified and apprehended.

The USS Cole attack had significant implications for U.S. naval policies and counterterrorism strategies. In the immediate aftermath, the U.S. Navy conducted a thorough review of its force protection measures and port security protocols. The findings highlighted vulnerabilities in the procedures for refueling and port visits, leading to the implementation of more stringent security measures. These included enhanced threat assessments, improved coordination with host nations, and increased vigilance during port calls.

The attack also underscored the evolving nature of terrorism and the need for a comprehensive approach to counterterrorism. The U.S. government recognized the need to address the root causes of terrorism, strengthen international cooperation, and improve intelligence sharing. The attack on the Cole was a precursor to the broader campaign against al-Qaeda that would intensify following the September 11, 2001, attacks on the World Trade Center and the Pentagon. The lessons learned from the Cole attack informed the development of new strategies and tactics for combating terrorism, including the use of precision strikes, special operations forces, and enhanced surveillance.

The geopolitical implications of the USS Cole attack were profound. The incident strained U.S.-Yemen relations, as it highlighted the presence of al-Qaeda operatives in the country and raised questions about the Yemeni government's ability to control terrorist activities within its borders. In response, the U.S. increased its engagement with Yemen, providing assistance to improve its counterterrorism capabilities and strengthen its security forces. This cooperation was part of a broader effort to combat terrorism in the Arabian Peninsula and other regions where al-Qaeda had a significant presence.

Despite the severe damage sustained in the attack, the USS Cole was eventually repaired and returned to service. The ship was transported back to the United States aboard the heavy-lift ship Blue Marlin and underwent extensive repairs at the Ingalls Shipbuilding yard, where it had been originally constructed. The repair process involved replacing damaged sections of the hull, overhauling the propulsion and electrical systems, and updating the ship's combat systems. The Cole re-entered service in 2002, demonstrating the resilience and determination of the U.S. Navy and its commitment to maintaining a strong and capable fleet.

In the years following the attack, the USS Cole continued to serve with distinction, participating in numerous deployments and operations around the world. The ship's return to active duty was a powerful symbol of defiance against terrorism and a testament to the sacrifices made by its crew. The memory of the sailors who lost their lives in the attack has been honored through various memorials and commemorations, including the USS Cole Memorial at Naval Station Norfolk and the annual remembrance ceremonies held by the ship's crew and the broader naval community.

The legacy of the USS Cole extends beyond its operational history. The attack had a lasting impact on the U.S. Navy's approach to force protection, shaping the development of new policies and practices designed to safeguard ships and personnel in an increasingly complex security environment. The incident also contributed to the evolution of U.S. counterterrorism strategy, highlighting the need for a proactive and multifaceted approach to combating terrorist threats.

In historical context, the USS Cole attack represents a pivotal moment in the global fight against terrorism. It served as a wake-up call for the United States and its allies, underscoring the importance of vigilance, preparedness, and international cooperation in addressing the challenges posed by non-state actors. The attack also reinforced the enduring principle that freedom and security come at a cost, and that the sacrifices of those who serve must be honored and remembered.

The story of the USS Cole is a poignant reminder of the resilience and bravery of the men and women of the U.S. Navy. The crew's response to the attack, their dedication to their ship and each other, and their commitment to overcoming adversity exemplify the highest ideals of naval service. The USS Cole continues to sail as a testament to their courage and a symbol of America's resolve in the face of terrorism.

# Chapter 43: USS Cyclops

The USS Cyclops (AC-4) was a Proteus-class collier of the United States Navy that became one of the most famous naval mysteries of the 20th century when it disappeared without a trace in March 1918 during World War I. This enigmatic loss of the vessel, along with its 309 crew members and passengers, remains one of the single largest losses of life in U.S. Naval history not directly involving combat. The circumstances surrounding the disappearance have given rise to numerous theories and speculations, making the USS Cyclops a subject of enduring intrigue and speculation.

The USS Cyclops was built by William Cramp & Sons of Philadelphia. Laid down on August 7, 1910, and launched on May 7, 1910, the ship was commissioned into the Navy on May 1, 1917. As a collier, its primary function was to transport coal, which was the primary fuel for naval ships at the time, although it could also carry other bulk cargo. The Cyclops was 542 feet (165 meters) long, 65 feet (20 meters) wide, and had a gross tonnage of 19,360 tons. The ship was powered by two steam engines, giving it a top speed of 15 knots. It was equipped with four large holds that could carry up to 12,500 tons of coal or other cargo, making it a vital asset for resupplying the fleet.

During its operational career, the USS Cyclops served various roles, including transporting coal and other supplies to American and Allied forces stationed around the globe. When the United States entered World War I in April 1917, the ship's role became even more critical, as it was tasked with supporting the war effort by ensuring the steady supply of fuel and materials necessary for naval operations.

The final voyage of the USS Cyclops began on January 9, 1918, when the ship departed from Norfolk, Virginia, under the command of Lieutenant Commander George W. Worley. The ship's mission was to transport manganese ore, a vital material used in steel production, from Brazilian ports to Baltimore, Maryland. The Cyclops made stops in Rio de Janeiro and Bahia, Brazil, to load the ore and took on additional passengers, including sailors and civilians.

The ship departed from Rio de Janeiro on February 16, 1918, and stopped in Bahia on February 20, 1918, for additional supplies and to make final preparations for its voyage north. The Cyclops left Bahia on February 22, 1918, with an estimated total of 309 crew members and passengers on board, heading towards Baltimore. The last known communication from the ship was a routine radio message sent on March 4, 1918, when it was off the coast of Barbados in the Caribbean Sea. After this, the USS Cyclops and everyone on board vanished without a trace.

The disappearance of the USS Cyclops has baffled historians, naval experts, and conspiracy theorists for over a century. Despite extensive searches and investigations conducted by the Navy and other agencies, no wreckage, debris, or bodies were ever found. This complete lack of physical evidence has fueled a wide range of theories and speculations about what might have happened to the ship and its crew.

One of the most plausible theories is that the USS Cyclops was lost due to structural failure or mechanical issues. The ship was known to have experienced problems with its engines and hull before its final voyage. Some reports suggest that the Cyclops was overloaded with manganese ore, which could have caused it to become unstable or even break apart in rough seas. Additionally, the ship's design, with its large open holds and relatively narrow beam, may have made it susceptible to structural stresses and potential capsizing.

Weather conditions have also been considered a potential factor in the ship's disappearance. The Cyclops was sailing through an area known for its unpredictable weather and frequent storms. It is possible that the ship encountered a severe storm or hurricane, which could have overwhelmed its defenses and caused it to sink. However, no records of significant weather disturbances in the area at the time of the ship's last known position have been found, leaving this theory inconclusive.

Another theory is that the USS Cyclops was sunk by enemy action. During World War I, German U-boats and surface raiders operated in the Atlantic and Caribbean, targeting Allied shipping. Some have speculated that the Cyclops was torpedoed or attacked by a German submarine or raider. However, no German records or logs from the period contain any mention of an engagement with the Cyclops, and no wreckage consistent with a torpedo attack has ever been found.

Sabotage and mutiny have also been suggested as possible explanations. Lieutenant Commander Worley, the ship's captain, was known to be a controversial and unpopular figure among the crew. Born Johann Frederick Wichmann in Germany, he had immigrated to the United States and changed his name. Some have speculated that Worley might have been involved in sabotage or espionage, or that a mutiny occurred on board. However, there is no concrete evidence to support these claims, and they remain speculative.

The disappearance of the USS Cyclops has also given rise to more exotic and speculative theories, including those involving supernatural or extraterrestrial phenomena. Some have suggested that the ship fell victim to the so-called Bermuda Triangle, a region of the Atlantic Ocean reputed for mysterious disappearances of ships and aircraft. Others have proposed that the ship was abducted by aliens or swallowed by a giant sea creature. These theories, while popular in certain circles, lack any scientific basis and are generally regarded as fringe speculation.

In the years following the disappearance, the U.S. Navy conducted several investigations to try to determine the fate of the USS Cyclops. These investigations included interviews with survivors from other ships, reviews of ship logs and weather reports, and searches of the ship's likely route. Despite these efforts, no conclusive evidence was found to explain the ship's disappearance. The loss of the Cyclops was a profound tragedy for the families of the crew and passengers, as well as a significant blow to the Navy during a critical period of World War I.

The mystery of the USS Cyclops has had a lasting impact on naval history and maritime lore. The ship's disappearance has been the subject of numerous books, articles, documentaries, and even fictional stories. It remains one of the most enduring maritime mysteries, often cited alongside other famous disappearances like the Mary Celeste and the Flight 19 incident.

In addition to its historical and cultural significance, the disappearance of the USS Cyclops has had practical implications for naval operations and safety. The incident highlighted the potential risks associated with large bulk carriers and the need for stringent safety standards and protocols. The Navy and other maritime organizations have since implemented more rigorous inspection and maintenance procedures for ships, as well as improved communication and tracking technologies to enhance the safety and security of maritime operations.

The legacy of the USS Cyclops is also a reminder of the sacrifices made by those who serve in the military, particularly during times of war. The ship's loss and the lives of its crew and passengers are commemorated through various memorials and remembrance ceremonies. These tributes honor the bravery and dedication of the men and women who served on the Cyclops and underscore the importance of remembering and learning from history.

# Chapter 44: RMS Republic

The RMS Republic, often referred to as the "Millionaires' Ship," was a steam-powered ocean liner that met a tragic end in 1909. Built by Harland and Wolff in Belfast for the White Star Line, the ship was launched on February 26, 1903. It was initially intended to serve as a luxurious transatlantic passenger liner, catering to the wealthy and affluent, as well as providing essential services for emigrants and other travelers between Europe and North America. The story of the RMS Republic is notable not only for its opulence and service but also for the dramatic events surrounding its sinking, which resulted in the largest maritime rescue operation of its time and gave birth to enduring rumors about lost treasure.

The RMS Republic was a marvel of early 20th-century engineering and design. Measuring 570 feet in length and 67 feet in width, the ship had a gross tonnage of 15,378 tons. It was powered by two triple-expansion steam engines, driving twin screws that could propel the vessel at a speed of up to 16 knots. The ship's interior was lavishly appointed, with opulent first-class accommodations, grand dining salons, and elegant public spaces designed to attract wealthy passengers. The ship also featured modern amenities such as electric lighting, wireless telegraphy, and spacious cabins, making it one of the most comfortable and advanced liners of its time.

The Republic embarked on its maiden voyage from Liverpool to Boston on October 17, 1903. It quickly became known for its luxurious accommodations and impeccable service, catering to a clientele that included some of the wealthiest and most influential people of the era. The ship operated on the lucrative transatlantic route, connecting major European ports with New York and other North American destinations. Over the next few years, the Republic transported thousands of passengers across the Atlantic, earning a reputation for safety, reliability, and comfort.

The fateful voyage that would seal the RMS Republic's place in maritime history began on January 22, 1909, when the ship departed from New York bound for Gibraltar and Mediterranean ports. On board were 742 passengers and crew, including a significant number of wealthy individuals and their families, along with valuable cargo and mail. The ship's captain, William Inman Sealby, was an experienced mariner with a reputation for competence and professionalism. As the Republic made its way across the North Atlantic, it encountered foggy conditions, a common hazard in the region during winter months.

In the early hours of January 23, 1909, the RMS Republic was navigating through dense fog approximately 26 miles off the coast of Nantucket, Massachusetts. Visibility was severely limited, and despite the use of the ship's foghorn and careful navigation, a collision occurred at 5:47 AM. The Italian liner SS Florida, traveling at high speed, emerged from the fog and struck the Republic on its port side, just aft of the engine room. The impact caused a massive breach in the Republic's hull, leading to severe flooding and the immediate death of three passengers who were asleep in their cabins near the point of impact.

The collision set off a chaotic and dramatic chain of events. Captain Sealby and his crew quickly assessed the damage and realized that the Republic was taking on water at an alarming rate. Recognizing the severity of the situation, Sealby ordered the ship's wireless operator, Jack Binns, to send out distress signals using the Marconi wireless telegraphy system, a relatively new technology at the time. Binns' repeated SOS signals were among the first ever to be transmitted in a maritime emergency, marking a significant moment in the history of wireless communication.

The SOS signals were picked up by several nearby vessels, including the White Star Line's own RMS Baltic, the SS Republic, and the US Coast Guard cutter Gresham. The RMS Baltic, under the command of Captain J.B. Ranson, was the first to respond, altering its course to assist the stricken Republic. Meanwhile, the SS Florida, which had also sustained significant damage in the collision, remained on the scene to provide assistance. Despite the chaos and confusion, the Republic's crew and passengers maintained remarkable composure and discipline.

As the Republic continued to flood, Captain Sealby made the difficult decision to abandon ship. Lifeboats were lowered, and passengers were carefully transferred from the listing Republic to the waiting SS Florida and other rescue vessels. The evacuation was conducted with remarkable efficiency, thanks in large part to the calm leadership of the officers and crew. Despite the challenging conditions, all but six of the Republic's passengers and crew were safely evacuated, making the rescue operation one of the most successful and well-coordinated in maritime history.

By the afternoon of January 23, the RMS Baltic arrived on the scene and took on the majority of the Republic's passengers, providing them with food, medical care, and accommodation. Meanwhile, Captain Sealby and a small contingent of volunteers remained aboard the Republic, attempting to save the ship. They worked tirelessly to pump out water and stabilize the vessel, but their efforts were ultimately in vain. The flooding continued unabated, and the Republic's condition worsened.

On January 24, 1909, as the situation became increasingly dire, Captain Sealby and his remaining crew were forced to abandon the Republic. The ship sank slowly over the course of several hours, finally disappearing beneath the waves at approximately 8:00 PM. The exact location of the wreck is believed to be at a depth of around 270 feet, off the coast of Nantucket. The loss of the RMS Republic was a significant blow to the White Star Line, both financially and reputationally, but the successful rescue operation was widely praised and highlighted the importance of wireless communication in maritime safety.

The sinking of the RMS Republic also gave rise to enduring rumors and legends about lost treasure. According to some accounts, the ship was carrying a substantial amount of gold and other valuables, intended as a financial transaction for the U.S. Navy or other entities. Estimates of the treasure's value vary widely, with some suggesting it could be worth millions of dollars in today's currency. Over the years, numerous salvage operations have been conducted in an attempt to recover the alleged treasure, but none have been successful. The exact nature and whereabouts of any treasure that may have been aboard the Republic remain speculative and unproven.

In addition to the treasure legend, the story of the RMS Republic has been immortalized in various books, articles, and documentaries. The ship's dramatic sinking, combined with the successful rescue operation and the mystery of the lost treasure, has captivated the imagination of maritime enthusiasts and historians for over a century. The Republic's legacy is a testament to the bravery and professionalism of its crew, the importance of technological advancements in maritime safety, and the enduring allure of unsolved mysteries.

The wreck of the RMS Republic lies at the bottom of the Atlantic Ocean, largely forgotten except by those who continue to seek the rumored treasure. It serves as a poignant reminder of the perils faced by early 20th-century mariners and the dramatic events that can unfold on the high seas. The story of the RMS Republic is a rich tapestry of human endeavor, technological innovation, and the relentless pursuit of discovery, encapsulating the spirit of an era when ocean liners were the lifeblood of transatlantic travel and commerce.

# Chapter 45: SS El Faro

The SS El Faro was a United States-flagged cargo ship that tragically sank on October 1, 2015, during Hurricane Joaquin, resulting in the loss of all 33 crew members. The disaster marked one of the deadliest U.S. maritime tragedies in recent history and raised significant questions about maritime safety, weather forecasting, and decision-making processes in the face of natural disasters. The story of the SS El Faro is a complex and sobering tale of human error, mechanical failure, and the relentless power of nature.

The SS El Faro was built in 1974 by Sun Shipbuilding and Drydock Company in Chester, Pennsylvania. Originally named Puerto Rico, the ship underwent several name changes and modifications throughout its service life. By the time of its final voyage, El Faro was a roll-on/roll-off (RO/RO) cargo ship, designed to transport vehicles and containerized cargo. The vessel was 790 feet long, with a beam of 94 feet, and a gross tonnage of 31,515 tons. It was powered by a single steam turbine engine capable of producing 22,000 horsepower, driving a single propeller that could propel the ship at speeds up to 22 knots.

Operated by TOTE Maritime, El Faro primarily served the trade route between Jacksonville, Florida, and San Juan, Puerto Rico. This route was crucial for supplying goods and materials to Puerto Rico, especially in the wake of the island's economic challenges. The ship's crew consisted of experienced mariners, many of whom had spent years working on similar vessels and routes. The captain, Michael Davidson, had over 20 years of experience with TOTE Maritime and was well-regarded by his colleagues and superiors.

On September 29, 2015, El Faro departed from Jacksonville on what would be its final voyage. The ship was carrying a mix of containerized cargo, vehicles, and trailers, along with a crew of 28 U.S. citizens and five Polish nationals. At the time of departure, Hurricane Joaquin was a tropical storm brewing in the Caribbean, with forecasts indicating it could strengthen and potentially impact the ship's intended route. Captain Davidson and his crew were aware of the storm and monitored weather updates closely.

As El Faro sailed southeast, Hurricane Joaquin intensified rapidly, becoming a Category 3 hurricane by September 30. Despite the worsening conditions, Captain Davidson chose to maintain the ship's course toward San Juan, believing they could navigate around the storm's projected path. The decision to proceed was influenced by several factors, including the captain's confidence in his ship's capabilities, pressure to maintain the delivery schedule, and initial weather forecasts that underestimated the storm's intensity and trajectory.

By the early hours of October 1, 2015, El Faro found itself perilously close to the eye of Hurricane Joaquin, which had now intensified to a Category 4 hurricane with sustained winds of 130 miles per hour. The ship encountered massive waves, powerful winds, and torrential rain, severely hampering its ability to navigate and maintain stability. At approximately 5:30 AM, the ship's main propulsion system failed, leaving it adrift in the heart of the storm. The crew made desperate attempts to restore power and stabilize the vessel, but the situation quickly became dire.

The last known communication from El Faro came at 7:20 AM when Captain Davidson reported to TOTE Maritime that the ship had lost propulsion, was listing heavily to starboard, and was taking on water. Despite the crew's efforts to contain the flooding and restore power, the ship continued to list and eventually capsized, sinking into the depths of the Atlantic Ocean. All 33 crew members perished in the disaster, making it one of the deadliest U.S. maritime accidents in recent memory.

The sinking of El Faro triggered extensive investigations by the U.S. Coast Guard, the National Transportation Safety Board (NTSB), and other agencies. These investigations aimed to uncover the causes of the disaster, assess the decision-making processes of the captain and crew, and evaluate the effectiveness of the ship's design, maintenance, and safety procedures. The investigations involved analyzing the ship's data recorders, conducting interviews with TOTE Maritime personnel, and reviewing weather forecasts and communications.

One of the critical findings of the investigations was the failure of the ship's main propulsion system, which left El Faro vulnerable and unable to maneuver in the face of the hurricane. The exact cause of the propulsion failure remains unclear, but it is believed to have resulted from a combination of mechanical issues, flooding in the engine room, and the ship's extreme list. The loss of propulsion was a catastrophic event that sealed the fate of El Faro and its crew.

The investigations also highlighted significant lapses in the decision-making process of Captain Davidson. While he was an experienced and respected mariner, his decision to proceed into the path of a rapidly intensifying hurricane was heavily criticized. The NTSB report suggested that the captain's reliance on outdated weather forecasts, underestimation of the storm's severity, and failure to heed the concerns of his crew contributed to the tragedy. The report also emphasized the importance of effective bridge resource management and the need for captains to prioritize safety over schedules and commercial pressures.

Another critical aspect of the investigations was the assessment of the ship's design and maintenance. El Faro, being over 40 years old at the time of its sinking, had undergone several modifications and retrofits during its service life. The NTSB and Coast Guard examined whether the ship's age, structural integrity, and maintenance practices played a role in the disaster. While the ship was deemed seaworthy and compliant with regulations, the investigations revealed areas where maintenance and safety standards could have been improved, particularly concerning watertight integrity and the condition of critical machinery.

The role of TOTE Maritime in the disaster was also scrutinized. The investigations examined the company's policies, practices, and oversight mechanisms to determine whether they contributed to the events leading up to the sinking. The findings indicated that while TOTE Maritime had established safety protocols and procedures, there were deficiencies in how these were implemented and monitored. The company faced criticism for not providing more up-to-date weather information to the captain and for not having more robust systems in place to assess and mitigate risks associated with severe weather.

In response to the findings of the investigations, several recommendations were made to enhance maritime safety and prevent similar tragedies in the future. These recommendations included improving weather forecasting and communication systems, enhancing training and protocols for bridge resource management, and ensuring stricter adherence to maintenance and safety standards for aging vessels. The tragedy of El Faro underscored the need for a comprehensive approach to maritime safety that integrates technology, training, and rigorous oversight.

The sinking of El Faro had a profound impact on the maritime community and the families of the lost crew members. The tragedy prompted a reevaluation of industry practices and regulations, leading to several reforms aimed at improving safety and reducing the risks associated with maritime transportation. It also highlighted the bravery and dedication of mariners who face immense challenges and dangers in their work, often under extreme conditions.

Memorials and tributes were established to honor the memory of the 33 crew members who lost their lives. The maritime community, along with the families and friends of the victims, came together to remember their loved ones and advocate for stronger safety measures to protect future generations of seafarers. The legacy of El Faro serves as a reminder of the importance of vigilance, preparedness, and the relentless pursuit of safety in the maritime industry.

# Chapter 46: MV Sewol

The sinking of the MV Sewol is one of the most tragic and impactful maritime disasters in recent history, occurring on April 16, 2014. This South Korean ferry capsized and sank off the country's southwestern coast, leading to the death of 304 passengers, most of whom were high school students on a school trip. The incident not only exposed significant lapses in safety and regulatory oversight but also had profound social and political repercussions in South Korea, shaking the nation to its core.

The MV Sewol was a 6,825-ton vessel, originally built in Japan in 1994 and later purchased by the South Korean company Chonghaejin Marine Company in 2012. The ferry was designed to carry both passengers and cargo, with a capacity of 921 passengers and over 150 vehicles. Following its acquisition, the vessel underwent modifications, including the addition of extra passenger cabins and cargo space, which increased its gross tonnage and altered its balance and stability. These modifications, carried out without thorough regulatory oversight, played a crucial role in the disaster.

On April 15, 2014, the MV Sewol set sail from Incheon, heading towards Jeju Island. The vessel carried 476 people, including 325 students from Danwon High School, 14 teachers, and a mix of other passengers and crew. The journey was supposed to be a routine trip, offering students a memorable outing to the scenic island. However, the ferry was heavily overloaded, carrying more than three times the recommended weight of cargo, which was poorly secured. This overloading severely compromised the vessel's stability, a fact compounded by the illegal modifications made to the ship.

The following morning, around 8:50 AM, the ferry began to encounter trouble as it navigated through the Maenggol Channel. The waters were known for their strong currents, but the weather was calm and visibility was good. Despite this, the Sewol began to list sharply to starboard at around 8:50 AM. Investigations later revealed that the ship made a sharp turn, which likely caused the poorly secured cargo to shift, exacerbating the list and making it irrecoverable. The exact cause of the abrupt turn remains unclear, with some attributing it to a steering error or sudden maneuver to avoid an obstacle.

As the ferry began to capsize, confusion and panic ensued on board. The crew, including the captain, Lee Joon-seok, delayed issuing an evacuation order, instructing passengers to stay in their cabins and follow the ship's public announcement system. This directive proved fatal, as passengers who remained inside were trapped when the vessel continued to list and eventually capsized. The captain and several crew members were among the first to abandon ship, failing to follow maritime protocols that dictate the crew should ensure the safety of passengers before evacuating themselves.

The Korean Coast Guard and other vessels quickly responded to the distress signals sent out by the Sewol. Despite the rapid response, the rescue operations were hampered by the chaotic state of the listing ship and the difficulty of accessing trapped passengers. Many of the initial rescue efforts focused on saving those who had jumped or fallen into the water. Divers faced significant challenges in entering the submerged parts of the vessel due to strong currents, poor visibility, and the complex layout of the ship.

Over the following days, rescue operations transitioned into a grim recovery mission as hopes of finding survivors dwindled. The South Korean government deployed a massive search and rescue operation involving naval and civilian divers, ships, and aircraft. The nation watched in anguish as the bodies of young students were recovered from the wreckage. The emotional toll on the families, the school community, and the broader public was immense.

The aftermath of the MV Sewol disaster sparked widespread outrage and calls for accountability. Investigations revealed numerous failures and instances of negligence. The ferry had been improperly modified and overloaded, and safety inspections had been lax. Furthermore, the crew's training and response were severely inadequate, as evidenced by their failure to properly manage the emergency and prioritize passenger safety. The captain and several crew members were arrested and charged with gross negligence and abandonment.

The South Korean government's handling of the disaster also came under intense scrutiny. Families of the victims and the public criticized the government's slow and disorganized response to the emergency. There were accusations of corruption and regulatory failures that allowed the ferry to operate despite its unsafe condition. President Park Geun-hye faced significant political backlash, with her administration accused of mishandling the crisis and failing to enforce necessary safety regulations.

In response to the tragedy, the South Korean government launched comprehensive reforms aimed at improving maritime safety and regulatory oversight. The Korean Coast Guard underwent restructuring, and new laws were enacted to ensure stricter enforcement of safety standards for passenger vessels. The disaster also led to the creation of the Ministry of Public Safety and Security, intended to coordinate disaster response efforts more effectively.

The emotional impact of the MV Sewol disaster resonated deeply across South Korea. The nation mourned the loss of so many young lives, and the disaster became a symbol of broader societal issues, including the perceived failures of government and corporate accountability. Memorials and vigils were held across the country, and the yellow ribbon became a poignant symbol of remembrance and solidarity with the victims and their families.

The legal proceedings following the disaster saw Captain Lee Joon-seok sentenced to life in prison for his actions, while other crew members received varying sentences for their roles in the tragedy. The owner of Chonghaejin Marine Company, Yoo Byung-eun, was also sought by authorities for his responsibility in the unsafe operation of the ferry. His mysterious disappearance and subsequent discovery of his body added another layer of intrigue and controversy to the case.

In the years since the disaster, the South Korean public has continued to seek justice and reforms. The Sewol tragedy has been a catalyst for ongoing debates about safety, governance, and the responsibilities of corporations and the state. Annual commemorations and continued activism by the victims' families have kept the memory of the disaster alive, ensuring that the lessons learned are not forgotten.

The sinking of the MV Sewol also had a significant impact on South Korean culture and media. The disaster was extensively covered by both domestic and international media, leading to a flood of documentaries, films, and books exploring the events and their aftermath. These works have played a crucial role in shaping public perception and understanding of the disaster, highlighting the human stories behind the tragedy and the need for systemic change.

# Chapter 47: MV Rabaul Queen

The MV Rabaul Queen was a passenger ferry operated by Rabaul Shipping in Papua New Guinea. The ferry sank on February 2, 2012, in the Solomon Sea, off the coast of the Morobe Province, resulting in one of the worst maritime disasters in the region's history. The tragedy claimed the lives of approximately 172 people, highlighting significant issues regarding maritime safety standards, regulatory oversight, and emergency preparedness in Papua New Guinea's maritime industry. This catastrophic event led to a profound examination of the practices of shipping companies and the effectiveness of the country's maritime regulatory framework.

The MV Rabaul Queen was built in 1983 in Japan and operated there before being acquired by Rabaul Shipping in 1998. The vessel was a roll-on/roll-off (RoRo) ferry, a type of ship designed to carry passengers and vehicles. With a gross tonnage of 259 tons, a length of 47 meters, and a beam of 10 meters, the Rabaul Queen was capable of carrying around 350 passengers, although it often exceeded this capacity. The ferry provided a crucial service, connecting various coastal towns and cities in Papua New Guinea, where maritime transport is a vital part of the transportation infrastructure due to the country's challenging terrain and limited road networks.

On January 31, 2012, the Rabaul Queen departed from Kimbe, West New Britain, bound for Lae, the second-largest city in Papua New Guinea. The voyage was part of its regular route, which included stops at various ports along the northern coast of New Britain and the eastern coast of New Guinea. The ferry was carrying a mix of passengers, including students, businesspeople, and families, as well as cargo. Reports indicated that the vessel was overcrowded, with over 350 passengers on board, exceeding its safe carrying capacity.

As the Rabaul Queen approached the final leg of its journey, it encountered severe weather conditions. The region was affected by a tropical storm, which brought strong winds and rough seas. Despite these hazardous conditions, the ferry continued its voyage, a decision that would later be heavily criticized. In the early hours of February 2, 2012, as the ferry was navigating the treacherous waters of the Solomon Sea, it was hit by powerful waves and began to take on water. The situation quickly escalated as the vessel started to list and eventually capsized, sinking rapidly.

The disaster struck with little warning, leaving passengers and crew in a state of panic and confusion. Many passengers were trapped inside the ferry as it capsized, while others were thrown into the rough seas. The chaos was exacerbated by the lack of adequate life-saving equipment and the poor state of the ferry's emergency preparedness. Survivors later recounted harrowing experiences of struggling to stay afloat and clinging to debris in the turbulent waters.

Rescue efforts were launched immediately after the ferry's distress signals were received. The Papua New Guinea Maritime Safety Authority (PNGMSA), along with the Australian Maritime Safety Authority (AMSA) and various private vessels, coordinated the search and rescue operations. Helicopters, planes, and ships were dispatched to the scene to search for survivors. Over the course of several days, rescuers managed to save approximately 246 people, many of whom were found clinging to life rafts or floating in the water. Despite these efforts, the bodies of many victims were never recovered, and the final death toll was estimated to be around 172.

The sinking of the Rabaul Queen triggered an immediate outcry and calls for a thorough investigation into the circumstances of the disaster. The Papua New Guinea government established a Commission of Inquiry to examine the incident, focusing on the factors that led to the sinking, the actions of the ship's operators, and the effectiveness of the maritime regulatory framework. The inquiry aimed to provide answers to the grieving families and to recommend measures to prevent similar tragedies in the future.

The Commission of Inquiry's findings, released later in 2012, painted a grim picture of negligence, regulatory failures, and systemic issues within the country's maritime industry. The inquiry revealed that the Rabaul Queen was significantly overloaded at the time of the sinking, carrying far more passengers than its designed capacity. This overloading not only compromised the vessel's stability but also severely hampered the evacuation process when the disaster struck. Additionally, the ferry was found to be in poor condition, with critical safety equipment either missing or not functioning properly.

One of the most damning aspects of the inquiry's findings was the failure of Rabaul Shipping to heed weather warnings and the poor judgment exercised in continuing the voyage despite the adverse weather conditions. The inquiry highlighted that the decision to sail in such dangerous conditions was influenced by commercial pressures and a disregard for passenger safety. The ship's captain and crew were criticized for their inadequate response to the emergency, which contributed to the high casualty rate.

The inquiry also scrutinized the role of the National Maritime Safety Authority (NMSA), the regulatory body responsible for overseeing maritime safety in Papua New Guinea. The NMSA was found to have been ineffective in enforcing safety standards and monitoring the operations of shipping companies. The lack of rigorous inspections and the failure to ensure compliance with safety regulations allowed substandard vessels like the Rabaul Queen to operate, putting passengers at significant risk.

In response to the Commission of Inquiry's findings, the Papua New Guinea government took several measures to address the shortcomings in the maritime industry. These included stricter enforcement of safety regulations, mandatory safety audits for passenger vessels, and enhanced training programs for ship crews. The government also committed to improving the infrastructure and resources available to the NMSA to ensure better oversight and enforcement of maritime safety standards.

The legal repercussions for Rabaul Shipping were significant. The company's owner, Peter Sharp, and several senior executives faced criminal charges related to the disaster, including manslaughter and negligence. The legal proceedings were protracted and complex, with the company and its executives maintaining their innocence and attributing the disaster to an act of God. However, the overwhelming evidence of negligence and regulatory failures resulted in convictions and substantial financial penalties for the company.

The sinking of the Rabaul Queen also had broader implications for maritime safety in the Pacific region. The disaster prompted regional organizations and neighboring countries to review their own maritime safety practices and regulatory frameworks. There was a renewed emphasis on regional cooperation to enhance maritime safety standards and to share best practices in vessel inspection, crew training, and emergency response.

For the families of the victims and the survivors, the sinking of the Rabaul Queen left an indelible mark. The trauma and loss experienced by those affected were profound, and many struggled with the emotional and psychological aftermath of the disaster. Community support groups and counseling services were established to provide assistance to the grieving families and survivors, helping them cope with their loss and begin the process of healing.

In the years following the disaster, efforts to commemorate the victims and honor their memory have continued. Memorial services and events are held annually to remember those who perished, and the story of the Rabaul Queen has been integrated into the broader narrative of maritime safety advocacy in Papua New Guinea. The disaster serves as a somber reminder of the importance of vigilance, accountability, and the unyielding pursuit of safety in the maritime industry.

The legacy of the MV Rabaul Queen is multifaceted, encompassing both the tragic loss of life and the subsequent improvements in maritime safety that emerged from the disaster. While the sinking exposed severe deficiencies in the industry's regulatory framework and operational practices, it also catalyzed meaningful changes aimed at preventing similar tragedies in the future. The lessons learned from the Rabaul Queen disaster continue to resonate within the maritime community, underscoring the critical importance of safety, regulation, and the protection of human life at sea.

# Chapter 48: HMS Eurydice

The HMS Eurydice was a 26-gun Royal Navy corvette launched in 1843 and converted to a training ship in 1877. Her tragic sinking in 1878 is one of the most infamous maritime disasters in British naval history. The ship, which was one of the last large sailing vessels built by the Royal Navy, met her end off the Isle of Wight, resulting in the loss of nearly all hands. This disaster had a significant impact on naval training practices and the Royal Navy as a whole.

HMS Eurydice was a 921-ton wooden-hulled sailing ship, typical of mid-19th century naval design. She was equipped with square rigging and carried a broadside of 26 guns. The vessel was constructed at Portsmouth Dockyard and launched on May 16, 1843. Throughout her service, Eurydice undertook various roles, including patrolling and escort duties, reflecting the versatile nature of corvettes in the Royal Navy's fleet. In 1877, Eurydice was repurposed as a training ship to provide practical seamanship training to young naval cadets. This role was vital as it prepared the next generation of sailors for the challenges of naval service, emphasizing sailing techniques, navigation, and discipline.

On March 6, 1878, the Eurydice departed from Bermuda, where she had been stationed for a training cruise in the West Indies. Commanded by Captain Marcus Augustus Stanley Hare, the ship carried 319 crew members and trainees. The voyage back to England was expected to take several weeks, and the Eurydice sailed smoothly across the Atlantic, navigating the typical challenges of such a journey, including variable weather and sea conditions. The ship approached the English Channel in late March, ready to complete her return journey to Portsmouth.

On March 24, 1878, as Eurydice neared the Isle of Wight, the weather appeared calm. However, this tranquility was deceptive, as sudden and severe changes in weather conditions were not uncommon in the region. At approximately 4:00 PM, the ship was caught in a sudden and fierce snowstorm. The combination of strong winds, heavy snow, and rapidly dropping temperatures created treacherous conditions. The crew attempted to reduce sail and stabilize the vessel, but the sudden shift in weather left little time to react effectively. The Eurydice, heeling over under the pressure of her full sail, was unable to right herself and quickly began to take on water.

The ship capsized and sank within minutes, trapping many of the crew and trainees below deck. The suddenness of the disaster meant that there was little chance for an organized evacuation. The icy waters further compounded the tragedy, as those who managed to escape the sinking vessel were subjected to near-freezing temperatures. The combination of cold water and hypothermia claimed the lives of most who had managed to leave the ship. Of the 319 men aboard, only two survived. The survivors, Charles Beauchamp and Sidney Fletcher, were rescued by local fishermen who had witnessed the disaster from shore. The enormity of the loss stunned the nation and sent shockwaves through the Royal Navy.

The sinking of the HMS Eurydice prompted an immediate inquiry into the causes of the disaster. The investigation focused on the weather conditions, the ship's handling, and the actions of the crew. It was determined that the sudden snowstorm, known as a squall, had been the primary cause of the sinking. The inquiry highlighted the difficulties of predicting such weather changes and the challenges of responding effectively in the limited time available. The report also noted that the ship had been sailing with her ports open, which allowed water to flood the lower decks rapidly. This design flaw, coupled with the sudden weather conditions, had made the sinking almost inevitable.

The Eurydice disaster had a profound impact on naval training and safety practices. One of the immediate responses was a review of training protocols and ship handling procedures, particularly in adverse weather conditions. The Royal Navy recognized the need for better training in weather prediction and response, emphasizing the importance of rapid and coordinated action during emergencies. The disaster also led to changes in ship design, particularly the practice of keeping ports closed during potentially hazardous conditions. The loss of so many young cadets underscored the need for improved safety measures and a more comprehensive understanding of maritime risks.

The Eurydice also entered popular culture and folklore, with numerous reports of ghostly apparitions of the ship being sighted near the Isle of Wight. These stories added a supernatural dimension to the already tragic tale, capturing the public's imagination and ensuring that the memory of the disaster remained alive in popular consciousness. The shipwreck itself became a subject of fascination for maritime historians and ghost enthusiasts alike. The Isle of Wight, known for its picturesque scenery and maritime history, became a place of pilgrimage for those intrigued by the ghostly legends associated with the Eurydice. The wreck of the ship remained a poignant underwater memorial, a stark reminder of the dangers faced by sailors and the unpredictable nature of the sea.

In the years following the disaster, several memorials were established to honor the memory of those who perished. A prominent memorial is located in St. Ann's Church, Portsmouth, where a plaque commemorates the officers, crew, and trainees who lost their lives. The memorial serves as a place of reflection and remembrance for the families of the victims and the wider naval community. Anniversaries of the disaster have been marked by ceremonies and services, ensuring that the sacrifice of those aboard the Eurydice is not forgotten.

The legacy of the HMS Eurydice disaster extends beyond the immediate changes to naval practices and training. It serves as a historical lesson in the importance of preparedness and the constant vigilance required in maritime operations. The disaster highlighted the unpredictable nature of the sea and the need for continual improvement in safety measures and training protocols. The Royal Navy's response to the Eurydice disaster helped shape future policies and practices, contributing to the development of more robust and resilient naval operations.

In contemporary times, the story of the HMS Eurydice continues to be studied and remembered. The shipwreck has been explored by divers, and artifacts recovered from the site provide tangible links to the past. Maritime historians and researchers continue to analyze the disaster, seeking to understand the full scope of the events and their impact on naval history. The Eurydice remains a significant case study in maritime disaster response and the evolution of naval safety practices.

# Chapter 49: SS Waratah

The SS Waratah was a passenger and cargo steamer built in 1908 by Barclay Curle & Co. Ltd. in Glasgow, Scotland, for the Blue Anchor Line. Named after the Australian floral emblem, the waratah, the ship was designed to serve the route between Europe and Australia, providing a crucial link for passengers and freight during a time when maritime travel was a primary means of long-distance transportation. The Waratah's mysterious disappearance in 1909, along with all 211 passengers and crew, remains one of the greatest maritime mysteries and has led to extensive speculation and numerous theories about what might have happened to the ill-fated vessel.

The SS Waratah was a significant vessel for its time, featuring modern design and engineering advancements. She was 500 feet long, 59.6 feet wide, and had a gross tonnage of 9,339 tons. Her twin quadruple-expansion steam engines enabled a top speed of 13 knots. The ship had accommodations for 750 passengers, with luxurious first-class quarters designed to attract wealthy travelers. The Waratah was launched with great expectations and was considered a state-of-the-art liner, exemplifying the era's advances in shipbuilding technology.

The Waratah set sail on her maiden voyage from London to Australia on November 5, 1908, under the command of Captain Joshua Ilbery, a seasoned mariner with extensive experience. The journey proceeded without major incidents, and the ship arrived in Sydney in January 1909. However, concerns about her stability and seaworthiness began to surface during this initial voyage. Some passengers reported that the Waratah had a tendency to roll excessively, and rumors circulated that the ship might be top-heavy. Despite these concerns, the vessel continued to operate on her designated route.

On July 1, 1909, the Waratah departed Durban, South Africa, for her return journey to London, with stops planned in Cape Town and other ports. The ship was carrying 211 passengers and crew, along with a cargo that included wool, frozen meat, and various other goods. The voyage initially proceeded uneventfully, but the Waratah encountered severe weather conditions as she approached the South African coast. On July 26, she arrived in Durban, where she took on additional cargo and passengers.

The Waratah left Durban on July 27, 1909, bound for Cape Town. She was last sighted by the crew of the SS Clan MacIntyre later that day. According to the Clan MacIntyre's captain, the Waratah appeared to be steaming steadily, albeit in deteriorating weather conditions. This sighting, which occurred approximately 14 miles off the coast, would be the last confirmed contact with the Waratah. The ship never reached Cape Town, and subsequent searches failed to find any trace of the vessel or her occupants.

The disappearance of the Waratah prompted a significant and immediate response. The British and Australian governments, along with the Blue Anchor Line, launched extensive search operations. Naval vessels, merchant ships, and even private yachts were mobilized to scour the seas and coastlines for any signs of the missing ship. These efforts, which included searches from the air and along the rugged coastline, were ultimately fruitless. No wreckage, bodies, or debris from the Waratah were ever recovered, deepening the mystery surrounding her fate.

Theories about the Waratah's disappearance have proliferated over the years, with explanations ranging from the plausible to the fantastical. One of the most prominent theories suggests that the ship may have capsized due to stability issues. Testimonies from passengers and crew on her earlier voyages indicated that the Waratah had a tendency to list and roll, suggesting that she might have been top-heavy or improperly ballasted. In rough seas, these stability problems could have led to a catastrophic capsize, causing the ship to sink rapidly with little chance for the crew or passengers to escape.

Another theory posits that the Waratah might have encountered a rogue wave or freak weather event. The South African coast is known for its unpredictable and severe weather conditions, including the infamous "Cape Rollers," large and powerful waves that can arise suddenly. If the Waratah had been struck by such a wave, she could have suffered critical damage or been overwhelmed, leading to her sinking. The lack of debris or survivors could be explained by the ship sinking intact and swiftly, with the wreck lying in deep and inaccessible waters.

Speculation also exists around the possibility of an onboard explosion. The Waratah was carrying a variety of goods, including potentially volatile materials such as chemicals and explosives. An accidental detonation of such cargo could have resulted in a rapid and catastrophic loss of the vessel. However, this theory is less supported by evidence, as no reports from the time indicated any signs of an explosion or related distress signals.

Some more outlandish theories include the notion of the Waratah encountering supernatural forces or being taken by aliens. These theories, while lacking any substantial evidence, reflect the broader cultural fascination with maritime mysteries and the human tendency to seek extraordinary explanations for inexplicable events. The Waratah's disappearance has become a part of maritime folklore, with stories and legends growing around the event over time.

In the years following the Waratah's disappearance, several expeditions have attempted to locate the wreck. These efforts have utilized advances in technology, including sonar mapping and underwater exploration vehicles, to search the ocean floor for clues. Despite these efforts, the precise location of the Waratah's final resting place remains unknown. The vast and treacherous waters off the South African coast, combined with the depth and complexity of the ocean terrain, have made the search exceptionally challenging.

The legacy of the SS Waratah extends beyond the mystery of her disappearance. The incident highlighted the need for rigorous safety and stability standards in ship design and construction. The inquiries and discussions that followed the Waratah tragedy contributed to changes in maritime regulations, emphasizing the importance of thorough stability testing and better safety protocols for passenger vessels. The Waratah's fate also underscored the inherent dangers of sea travel during an era when ships were the primary means of long-distance transportation.

The human cost of the Waratah disaster was profound, with 211 lives lost. The families of the passengers and crew were left to grapple with the uncertainty and grief of never knowing what had happened to their loved ones. The tragedy resonated deeply with the public, leading to memorials and commemorations that sought to honor those who perished. Over a century later, the Waratah's story continues to captivate and mystify, serving as a poignant reminder of the sea's unforgiving nature and the enduring allure of maritime mysteries.

# Chapter 50: SS Athenia

The SS Athenia was a British transatlantic passenger liner, built in 1922 by the Fairfield Shipbuilding and Engineering Company of Glasgow, Scotland, for the Anchor-Donaldson Line. She was the first Allied ship to be sunk by Germany in World War II, a mere hours after Britain declared war on Germany. The sinking of the Athenia on September 3, 1939, not only marked the beginning of the Battle of the Atlantic but also highlighted the vulnerabilities and risks faced by civilian maritime vessels during wartime. The tragedy claimed the lives of 117 passengers and crew, including American citizens, an event that had far-reaching diplomatic repercussions and influenced public opinion in the United States.

The SS Athenia was a notable ship of her time, with a gross tonnage of 13,465 tons, a length of 526 feet, and a beam of 66 feet. She was powered by steam turbines and could reach speeds of up to 15 knots. Designed to carry 1,500 passengers, the Athenia offered a range of accommodations, from first-class cabins to more economical third-class berths, making transatlantic travel accessible to a broader segment of the population. Her routes primarily included transatlantic crossings between the United Kingdom and North America, serving ports in Glasgow, Liverpool, and Montreal. Over her 17 years of service, the Athenia had built a reputation for reliability and comfort.

The outbreak of World War II drastically altered the landscape of maritime travel. On September 1, 1939, Germany invaded Poland, leading Britain and France to declare war on Germany on September 3. The Athenia, which had departed from Glasgow on September 1, 1939, bound for Montreal via Liverpool and Belfast, was caught in the middle of this rapidly escalating conflict. The ship, commanded by Captain James Cook, carried 1,103 passengers and 315 crew members. The passengers included British citizens, Europeans, Americans, and

Canadians, many of whom were attempting to escape the looming threat of war in Europe.

The Athenia's journey proceeded uneventfully until the evening of September 3, 1939. At around 7:38 PM, while the ship was approximately 250 miles off the coast of Ireland, she was spotted by the German submarine U-30, commanded by Oberleutnant Fritz-Julius Lemp. The U-30 had been patrolling the Atlantic as part of Germany's naval strategy to disrupt Allied shipping. Mistaking the Athenia for an armed merchant cruiser, Lemp ordered a torpedo attack. The submarine fired two torpedoes, one of which struck the Athenia on the port side near the engine room, causing a massive explosion. The ship immediately began to take on water and listed to port.

The aftermath of the torpedo strike was chaotic and harrowing. The explosion killed several passengers and crew instantly, and the rapidly sinking vessel created a scene of panic and confusion. The ship's crew, despite the dire circumstances, managed to launch lifeboats and began evacuating passengers. However, the suddenness of the attack and the damage to the ship made the evacuation extremely challenging. Many lifeboats were launched improperly or overturned in the rough seas, and the darkness further complicated the rescue efforts.

Distress signals were sent out, and several ships in the vicinity responded. The Norwegian tanker MS Knute Nelson, the American freighter SS City of Flint, the Swedish yacht Southern Cross, and the British destroyers HMS Electra, HMS Escort, and HMS Fame all came to the Athenia's aid. These vessels managed to rescue the majority of the passengers and crew from the lifeboats and the sinking ship. Despite the efforts of the rescuers, 98 passengers and 19 crew members lost their lives in the disaster. Among the victims were 28 Americans, an event that had significant implications for U.S. public opinion regarding the war.

The sinking of the Athenia had immediate and far-reaching consequences. News of the attack spread rapidly, causing outrage and condemnation around the world. The fact that a civilian passenger liner had been targeted in the early hours of the war highlighted the ruthlessness of the German naval strategy. The British government quickly denounced the attack as a blatant violation of international law, as the Athenia had been an unarmed civilian vessel. The Germans, initially unaware of the U-boat's involvement, denied responsibility and suggested that the British had sunk their own ship to draw the United States into the war.

The sinking had a profound impact on public opinion in the United States. Although the U.S. remained officially neutral at the time, the death of American citizens in the attack generated significant outrage and increased anti-German sentiment. President Franklin D. Roosevelt condemned the attack and emphasized the need for preparedness and support for the Allies. The event underscored the dangers faced by civilian ships and contributed to the U.S. government's decision to provide greater assistance to Britain and its allies, eventually leading to measures like the Lend-Lease Act.

In the immediate aftermath, the German government attempted to cover up the U-boat's involvement. The Kriegsmarine, unaware of Lemp's actions, issued statements denying that any of their submarines had attacked the Athenia. Lemp himself did not report the sinking, fearing repercussions for attacking a passenger ship. It was only after the war, during the Nuremberg Trials, that the full details of the incident emerged. The German naval command eventually acknowledged that U-30 had sunk the Athenia, attributing the attack to a mistake by Lemp, who believed he was targeting an armed enemy vessel.

The sinking of the Athenia also had a significant impact on maritime warfare strategies and policies. The incident highlighted the vulnerability of civilian ships and the need for better protection against submarine attacks. The Royal Navy and other Allied navies began to implement convoy systems more rigorously, where merchant ships would travel in groups escorted by warships to provide greater defense against U-boat attacks. This strategy proved to be a crucial element in the Battle of the Atlantic, helping to mitigate the threat posed by German submarines.

In the years following the sinking, several inquiries and investigations were conducted to determine the exact circumstances of the attack. The British Admiralty and the United States both conducted their own investigations, which concluded that the Athenia had been unlawfully targeted by a German submarine. The findings of these inquiries were used to bolster Allied propaganda efforts, emphasizing the barbarity of the German military tactics and the necessity of defeating the Axis powers.

The legacy of the SS Athenia and her tragic end remains a poignant chapter in maritime and wartime history. The ship's sinking is commemorated by various memorials and remembrances, honoring the victims and highlighting the broader impact of the event. The Athenia's story serves as a reminder of the perils faced by civilian mariners during wartime and the far-reaching consequences of military actions. The incident also underscores the complexities of naval warfare and the tragic loss of innocent lives that often accompanies conflict.

# Epilogue

As we draw our journey through "Historical Records of Maritime Tragedies" to a close, we find ourselves gazing back over a sea of stories that have both haunted and fascinated humankind for centuries. These tales are more than mere accounts of tragedy and loss; they are windows into the human condition, revealing our relentless pursuit of exploration, our unyielding courage in the face of adversity, and the mysteries that continue to elude our understanding.

The ocean, with its infinite horizons and unfathomable depths, remains a powerful metaphor for the unknown. It reminds us that despite our advancements in technology and navigation, there are still realms where nature reigns supreme, where the unpredictable and the inexplicable hold sway. The stories chronicled in this book are testament to the sea's enduring capacity to surprise and challenge us.

Throughout these chapters, we have encountered the spectrum of human emotion: the terror of impending doom, the desperation of those clinging to life in the face of overwhelming odds, the sorrow of lives and legacies lost to the deep. Yet, we have also seen remarkable acts of bravery, resilience, and ingenuity. These narratives underscore the duality of the sea—its potential for both creation and destruction.

The mysteries we have explored—from the eerie abandonment of the Mary Celeste to the enigma of the Bermuda Triangle—remind us that not all questions have answers. These unresolved stories serve as a humbling reminder of the limits of our knowledge and the enduring allure of the unknown. They fuel our imaginations and inspire future generations to seek out answers, to explore further, and to understand more deeply.

As we close this book, we honor the memories of those who have been lost to the ocean's depths. Their stories are not just chronicles of what was, but are also cautionary tales for the future. They remind us of the importance of vigilance, the need for continuous improvement in maritime safety, and the respect we must maintain for the natural world.

We also pay tribute to the survivors and to those who have risked their lives in rescue operations. Their courage and determination exemplify the best of humanity's spirit, illuminating the darkest of times with their resilience and hope.

"Historical Records of Maritime Tragedies" is more than a collection of historical events; it is a reflection on our relationship with the sea. It is a narrative of our quest to conquer the unknown, our occasional hubris, and our ultimate respect for the forces of nature. As we leave these pages, may we carry forward the lessons learned, the stories remembered, and the respect earned for the mighty oceans that continue to shape our world.

Thank you for embarking on this voyage with us. May these stories stay with you, reminding you of the vast, mysterious, and ever-changing world that lies beyond the shore.


The End.